THE ANATOMY OF THE CAT

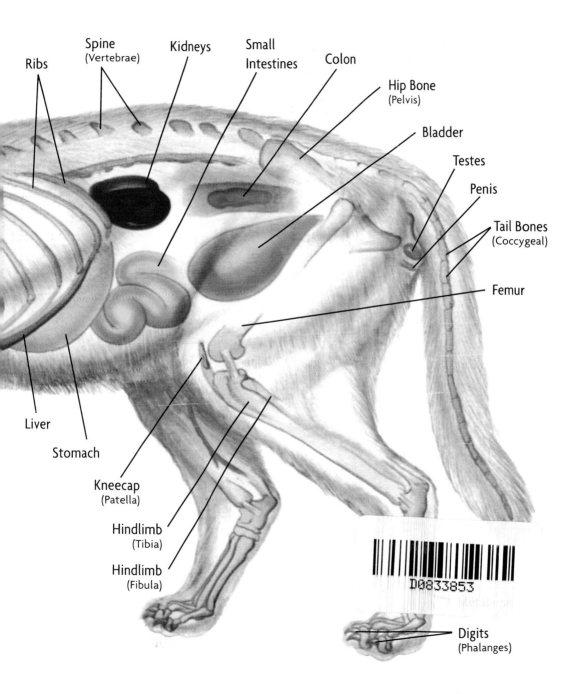

Ribs

Spine
(Vertebrae)

Kidneys

Small
Intestines

Colon

Hip Bone
(Pelvis)

Bladder

Testes

Penis

Tail Bones
(Coccygeal)

Femur

Liver

Stomach

Kneecap
(Patella)

Hindlimb
(Tibia)

Hindlimb
(Fibula)

Digits
(Phalanges)

DATE DUE

Manx Cat

By Victor H Radford

CONTENTS

PUBLISHED IN THE UNITED KINGDOM BY:

INTERPET
PUBLISHING

Vincent Lane, Dorking   Surrey RH4 3YX   England

ISBN 1-84286-049-6

PHOTO CREDITS
Photographs by Isabelle Francais and Alan Robinson
with additional photos provided by Michael W Brim,
Cat Fanciers' Association, Carolina Biological Supply,
Fleabusters Rx for Fleas, James R Hayden, RBP, Interpet,
Dwight R Kuhn, Dr Dennis Kunkel, Phototake,
Jean Claude Revy and W B Saunders Company.

The publisher wishes to thank
Dale L McKibben, Gale Thomas-Goodman and the rest of the
owners of the cats featured in this book.

History of the
MANX CAT

Boasting the world's oldest parliamentary government, called 'The Tynwald Court,' which dates back to Viking times when it was ruled by Norwegian Kings, the Isle of Man is the believed home of the famous Manx tailless cat. Man is steeped in mystery, superstitions and myths, so it is no surprise to find these are plentiful in respect to its famous cat.

FOLKLORE

Folklore and myths associated with the Manx breed are very much part of its romantic heritage. Such folklore is of relatively recent origin compared to the situation with traditional Manx folklore, which traces back many centuries. All of the folklore is related directly to the cat's tail, rather than being enshrined in deeper philosophical stories relating to wealth, changelings, witches, demons, fairies, goblins, giants and their like, which are found within most cat legends and myths.

Possibly the most well-known story is that the Manx was a normal-tailed cat until it was called to Noah's Ark. Determined to take a mouse with it, the result was it arrived late at the Ark. As it entered, Noah slammed the door

HOW DID THE MANX ARRIVE AT THE ISLE OF MAN?

Noah sailing o'er the seas, ran fast aground on Ararat.
His dog then sprang and took the tail from a pretty cat.
Puss through the window quick did fly,
And bravely through the waters swam.
Nor ever stopped till high and dry,
She landed on the Calf of Man*.
Thus tailless puss earned Mona's thanks,
And ever after was called a Manx.

*The Calf of Man is a small island off the Southwestern coast of the Isle of Man.

shut on its tail and ever after the cat's descendants had no tails.

Another story tells that Irish warriors cut the tails from the Manx cats to adorn their war helmets as lucky mascots. One day a mother cat decided to prevent this. She bit off the tails from each of her newborn kittens. Thereafter, there were no tails to be cut. In a variation of this, it was invading Vikings who cut the tails.

It was thought for many years that the Manx originated from the Orient, and that the Phoenicians took the cats to trade on the Isle of Man. In another story, the tailless cat was taken from the East to Spain. Years later, some of these cats were on board a ship of the defeated Spanish Armada when it was wrecked at Spanish Head, off the southern coast of Man, in 1588. The cats swam to the island, where they multiplied.

In another similar story, cats were on board a Russian ship that was wrecked off the Man coast during the late 1700s. An old folk story tells that a venomous serpent will attack any that tread on a cat's tail. To overcome this problem, the Islanders cut off the tails of their cats, thus making it safe to walk anywhere in Man. However, there are no snakes indigenous to that island.

In our final story, a greedy landowner decided to increase his wealth by applying a tax to all cats with tails. The owners, therefore,

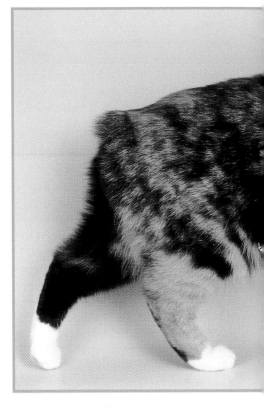

cut the tails off and the tax was avoided. Future offspring were born with no tails.

TRACING MANX HISTORY
Until the formation of the cat fancy as an organised hobby, the Manx was virtually unheard of. It was not regarded, for many years, as being anything special in Man itself. It was just another cat regarded as being a freak or runt. As a consequence, tracing its full history is impossible. A search for references to the breed in many guides to the Island published

The tailless cats from the Isle of Man have given rise to many colourful tales!

It must be assumed that the lack of tailless cat folklore at that time is indicative that there was no tailless cat. If there was, it is clear Waldron did not regard it as especially linked to the island, thus not worthy of mention.

In 1836, in a book entitled *A Six Days' Tour through The Isle of Man—By a Stranger* (thought to have been the architect John Welch) is found the following: 'Just beyond Glenmoji is Dalby...The uncontaminated Manx breed of men and cats may be found here in all purity. The most singular feature in the natural history of this country is, that the genuine aboriginal, orthodox cats have no tails; there is also a kind of poultry without this appendage, and they are both called, by way of distinction, 'runtties.' But as they intermarry with the more favoured English breeds, they have a quarter of a tail, half a tail, three quarters of a tail, and a full tail; according to some scale of deserts with which I am unacquainted.'

In 1841, the famous Man naturalist Edward Forbes wrote the 'Natural History' section in *Quiggin's Illustrated Guide and Visitor's Companion through The Isle of Man*. In this he states: 'The only remarkable quadruped peculiar to the Island, and of which it can boast, is the tail-less cat, an accidental variety of the common species, *Felis catus*.

during the 18th century has proved unproductive, other than in two instances. Given this fact, we must work with what we have in order to apply a time frame to its beginnings.

In 1726, George Waldron's *A Description of The Isle of Man* was first published. In this classic work, he gave a definitive description of the superstitions, ghosts and folklore of the Manx people. There is no mention of a tailless cat, nor is this mentioned within his comments on the animals of the island.

Frequently showing no trace of caudal vertebrae, and in others a merely rudimentary substitute for it.'

Using these points of reference, and in the absence of others yet unknown, it is probable that the Manx mutation first appeared between 1725 and about 1800. This allows a few years for it to have become established before gaining literary documentation.

In his book *The Manx Cat* (1965), D W Kerruish believed the breed was established centuries ago. However, the earliest reference he could find to the breed was in relation to cats

owned circa 1810 by the artist Joseph William Turner (1775–1841) that were purported to be from the Isle of Man.

ALTERNATIVE ORIGINS

Although the Manx breed has always been associated with the Isle of Man, this does not mean this was necessarily its birthplace. Mutations that are recorded, for example those creating the Devon and Cornish Rexes and the Scottish Fold, give us a definite point of reference in respect to both time and place.

But with mutations that preceded specific documentation, we can only refer to the time and place that we know of by association and reasonable calculation, rather than by definite fact. This holds true for all breeds, be they the Persian, the Siamese or any other comparable domestic feline.

With this in mind, it can be said that tailless cats were known in Cornwall from about the same time as they were being documented in Man. They were also known in France, the Crimea and elsewhere. They appear to have been numerous in the region of Kirkcudbright, in southwestern Scotland, during the early 1800s. It is here that it was claimed the tailless cat originated from a cross between a rabbit and a normal domestic cat. This is what accounted for its 'bunny hop' gait!

In each country, the lack of a

WHAT'S IN A NAME?

It is thought that the name 'Man' originates from the Saxon word *Mang*, which meant 'among,' referring to the island's position between England, Ireland, Scotland and Wales. However, for many years the islanders also used the names 'Maning' and 'Mann' to refer to their homeland, so it may be a shortening of one of these, or the Welsh name for it—*Manew*.

Man's Latin name is *Mona, Monapia* or *Monceda*. Mona, used by Julius Caesar, is an especially favoured name that the Romans applied variously to it—and to the island of Anglesey, lying near the Welsh coast. Many references using the name Mona can be found in Man's literature, in its place and street names and in its buildings.

The Manx is no 'cabbit.' The Manx's lack of a tail is attributed to genetic mutation as well as to man's mutilation, though surely not from a cross to the rabbit.

tail may have been from independent mutations, but they may also have been the original source of the Manx, which was subsequently transported to Man. The fact that the tailless cat was then isolated on a small island may have had favourable bearing on its propagation.

In 1846, in *The Christian Miscellany and Family Visitor*, an article describes the four races of cats. Our interest lies in the following: 'The tailless cats of Cornwall and the Isle of Man belong to the Chartreuse breed and are the ugliest of their kind, as the Angora are the handsomest.' The Chartreux is a French breed famed for its blue coat.

Experts of the day seemed uncertain as to the origins of the tailless cat. Some believed it came from Cornwall, whence it was taken to the Isle of Man. Others felt it originated in the Orient. However, in Oriental theories, it is probable that the experts were confusing the Manx with the Japanese Bobtail and other bobtails whose short tails derive from a quite separate mutation.

With respect to the comment that the Manx was ugly, this was not unique. The noted author Chas Ross stated in 1868, 'It is the most singular; its limbs are gaunt; its fur set close; its eyes staring and restless, and it has no tail....' Another author stated: 'A black Manx cat with its staring eyes and

Although today's cats are attractive in their own right, historically the Manx was never considered to be one of the feline beauties.

its stump of a tail is a most measly looking beast...It might be fitly the quadrupedal form in which ancient sorcerers were wont to cloth themselves on nocturnal excursions.'

Two points should be made in respect of these various quotes. First, those who probably owned the Manx in its earliest days were in the poorer strata of society. Many of their cats would be undernourished, and possibly not in good health—thus the 'staring eyes,' 'measly,' and 'gaunt' comments. Secondly, most educated Victorians tended to be very religious and stoic in their views. To them anything abnormal was an abomination normally best seen at, and left to, 'curio' exhibitions.

THE CAT FANCY BEGINS
On Thursday the 13th of July 1871, in the Crystal Palace, Sydenham, London, Harrison Weir, a noted artist and judge of poultry, staged the world's first major cat exhibition. He did this because he felt it would draw more favourable attention to cats, of which he had become a great lover. The show was an enormous success and it heralded the birth of the cat fancy as an organised hobby. Within a few years, the hobby spread to Continental Europe and America where it enjoyed the same success as in Britain.

One of the breeds on display at the show was a Manx. Fortunately, it appeared to be quite well cared for and did not appear to be the bedraggled feline described by earlier authors. In all, there were 170 cats on view. These included Siamese, Persian, Angora, Russian cats, British cats, a British wild cat, and cats said to be from other countries. Only six of these, including the Manx, subsequently became recognised breeds. The Manx was, therefore, one of only a select few of the 40+ current breeds that was present in the cat fancy from its very birth.

THE EARLY MANX
In 1889, Harrison Weir penned the first detailed description of the Manx in the form of a standard of points that was published in his book *Our Cats And All About Them*. In comparing his description with the present-day standard, it is clear the breed has changed in many features.

He states that the head was small (today medium to large), the neck long and thin (today short and thick), the ears small (today medium to tall), though earlier in the book he says they should be somewhat large. Shoulders to be narrow (today of good width), front legs medium length and thin (today short and of good substance).

The coat was required to be silky whereas today this should be coarser but still glossy. There was to be no tail, not even a stump—much as today—'but some true bred have a very short, thin, twisted tail that cannot be straightened, this allowable...' (today this would not be).

In general, the type called for by Weir in the 1890s was to change within a few years, as was that of his favoured British Shorthair. The trend over the years has been towards a heavier built, short-front-legged cat, this also being true of the British Shorthair, the breed that has had most influence on the Manx.

In his book, Weir states that a Mr Herbert Young of Harrogate owned a fine red female longhaired tailless cat that was bred from a Manx and a Persian. This he uses to illustrate the prepotency of the Manx tailless condition. This comment underscores the fact that in those days genetics was unknown to breeders. It also makes it clear that the gene for longhair was in the Manx breed from the earliest years, even though it gained no official recognition until relatively recent times.

MANX POPULARITY

By the early years of the 20th century, the cat fancy was well underway and the Manx slowly gained in popularity. From its probable origins among poor crofters, or their like, the breed

THE CRYSTAL PALACE SHOW

On 13 July 1871, an event took place that changed the world of the domestic cat. In the Crystal Palace at Sydenham, London, the world's first cat show took place. It was organised by Harrison Weir (1824–1906), a noted animal artist and great lover of cats.

The success of the cat show saw Weir become a noted cat judge and author. Today he is regarded as the 'father of the cat fancy.' In his later years he complained that Eastern cats were causing the demise of his beloved British Shorthairs. This did not endear him to Persian owners, whose cats were now beginning to dominate the hobby.

The Crystal Palace show attracted thousands of people, many of whom had never seen, or were not even aware of, some of the breed types. On display were many British Shorthairs, Siamese, Manx and a wild cat. Also present was a cat reputed to be direct from Persia. It was said to have a delightful personality and its colour was black, grey and white. White Persians were also on view. For many visitors these were by far the most impressive exhibits, with their pale blue eyes and flowing fur.

became quite fashionable.

This was certainly helped by the fact that in 1902 King Edward VII, seeing them during his tour of the Isle of Man, requested two to be sent to both Buckingham Palace and Balmoral. The cat fancy in its early years was very much a hobby strongly supported by nobility and the wealthy.

However, the term *popular* is relative. Although the Manx became well known, in total numbers it did not compare to the Persian or the Siamese. To a degree, its fortunes may also have been indirectly helped by 'fake' Manx. Once the breed gained popularity, the supply did not meet the demand so unscrupulous breeders on Man cut the tails from normal cats. These were sold as being true Manx. They became no more than items the Islanders could sell to tourists. As a consequence, the associated problems with the Manx were never evident in these fake Manx cats. But, of course, nor did they ever produce Manx offspring! The drain on the true Manx continued and in 1963 the Man government set up a breeding unit to ensure the breed's survival. This unit is no longer in operation.

With the passage of years, the breed became progressively less seen as more and more breeds arrived during, and since, the 1960s. It is thought that the breed

A popular pattern in the Manx is the brown tabby and white.

Producing healthy Manx kittens is more of a challenge than in most other breeds. Due to the Manx's genetics, breeding show-quality kittens is exceedingly difficult.

first started to attract attention in America during the 1930s. From that time onwards, it enjoyed increasing support to the point that its popularity there was far greater than in Britain and elsewhere.

THE MANX MUTATION

The source of the taillessness in the Manx is a dominant mutation that is lethal in the pure (homozygous) state and semi-lethal in the non-pure (heterozygous) state. The mutation affects the length of the spinal column and the caudal (tail) vertebrae. There may also be fusion between vertebrae. These changes may also affect the digestive system and the consequence of these changes may

include movement difficulties—the famed bunny hop of the breed being characteristic of mild signs—and bowel-function problems that result in the individual's not being able to control its motions.

When in the homozygous state, meaning a kitten that inherits the Manx gene from both parents, the result is prenatal death. This is the reason Manx to Manx matings always produce smaller than normal litters. A dominant mutation is one that only requires the gene to be in single dose to manifest its effect. It cannot, therefore, be carried hidden in the cat's genotype.

The effect on the tail is in one of four ways. If the tail is

POSSIBLE MATINGS

Genetically the Manx gene is symbolised by a capital M, non-Manx being a lowercase m. The results from the two possible matings is given for the benefit of potential breeders.

Mating 1

Mm × Mm = 25% MM (homozygous unborn offspring), 50% Mm (heterozygous Manx of the various tail types), 25% mm (homozygous non-Manx = Manx-bred)

Mating 2

Mm × mm = 50% Mm (heterozygous Manx of the various tail types), 50% mm (homozygous non-Manx = Manx-bred)

It can be mentioned that while the Manx-bred (mm) cat would appear to have little merit, and thus could be substituted by any shorthaired breed in a breeding programme, this overlooks two aspects. Firstly, feline registries do not allow the offspring of outcross breeds to be registered as Manx—they would be Manx variants.

Secondly, while the Manx-bred cat does not possess the Manx gene, it does possess all other of the Manx conformational requirements not affected by the gene. In other words, its head, ears, eyes, coat quality and colour, chest and front legs are the same. These will be passed on to its Manx offspring. Thus, the Manx-bred is important from a breeding perspective.

A final point on the mutation is that negative effects are normally manifest between birth and four months of age. Kittens should, therefore, be acquired only after this age to minimise the potential of obtaining a sickly kitten. An ethical breeder would not allow a kitten to be sold under this age.

completely absent, indicated by a slight depression where the tail would normally begin, this is called a Rumpy. This is the true Manx for exhibition purposes. If there is a short piece of bone at the tail root, which is immoveable, this is the Rumpy Riser and may also be exhibited in some associations.

If there is a short knob-like moveable tail, this is the Stumpy. The fourth type is the Longy or Longie, in which the tail is much longer but is shorter than the normal tail. The Stumpy and the Longy can only be exhibited in Any Other Variety (AOV) classes.

The mutant gene is variable in its effect, probably due to polygenic modifiers not yet understood. As a result of these, the various tail types may appear in the same litter.

It can be appreciated that breeding the Manx is very difficult and frustrating because of the low number of potential exhibition

The Manx is not the only tailless cat in the fancy. This is the Japanese Bobtail, an Asian tailless breed of considerable charm.

The Cymric is a longhaired Manx, a breed that has been around for nearly as long as the Manx itself.

THE LONGHAIRED MANX

Also called the Cymric (pronounced *kim-rick*), the Manx Longhair has existed within the Manx population almost since the time the breed was first identified. However, for many years the variety was ignored as a show cat and regarded as unwanted, being a vestige of breeding practice from the early years of the fancy.

But in Canada, about the 1960s, Althea Frahm (Lovebunny Cattery) was establishing the Manx Longhair as a breed unto itself. The variety was first shown about 1963 as a Manx Mutant with the American Cat Association (ACA), before being called the Cymric (the Gaelic word for 'Welsh').

It quickly gained recognition with the Canadian Cat Association and other registries. Many associations around the world now grant it recognition. Other than its longer coat, the breed is the same as the Shorthaired Manx.

The longhair gene is inherited as a recessive mutation quite independent of the Manx tailless gene. Unlike the Manx gene, both parents must carry a recessive gene for longhair in order for their offspring to display it. If only one parent has the gene, this will be passed to half of the offspring, who will carry it hidden in their genotype.

It has been claimed that the longhair mutation was spontaneous within the Manx breed. This is possible but unlikely, given that the records clearly show that other longhairs have been crossed with the Manx.

cats and the other effects. Breeders apply various policies in their programmes, the safest being to only pair a Manx with a Manx-bred individual, meaning one with a normal length tail.

FUTURE OF THE MANX

Were it not for the unfortunate deleterious health problems associated with the Manx gene, the breed would undoubtedly have been much more popular over the years, and its future would be more secure. However, the gene does make breeding

much more difficult than in most other breeds and results in low numbers of true Manx kittens.

But it is the health problems that may eventually see the breed go into demise. This will be more so in Britain and Europe than in America, where feline registries are more tolerant of the gene's negative side effects.

Presently, a number of associations retain the breed's register only on historical grounds. But this may not prove justifiable in the long-term future. The Manx is definitely a breed that needs to attract only the most devoted and knowledgeable of breeders in order to minimise potential problems.

This has been achieved to a high degree of success in recent decades. But whether it will be sufficient to maintain the breed in a cat fancy with changing values is another matter. If the Manx disappears from the show bench, it will bring to an end a breed that has gained undeniable fame throughout the world: a breed that helped to make the cat fancy the fascinating hobby it has become.

The length of the coat and length of the tail are to be considered when acquiring a Manx. It is vital that you acquire a Manx only from a reputable source.

A Portrait of the
MANX CAT

In its general appearance, the Manx is somewhat similar to the British Shorthair, though there are differences other than the fact that an exhibition Manx is tailless. Apart from its lack of tail, the Manx is distinguished from other cats by the fact that its rump is raised. This is a consequence of its rear legs being longer than those of other breeds in relation to the length of the front legs. It is its long back legs that gave the breed its famed, but unwanted, 'bunny hop' gait.

The Manx is available in both short- and longhaired forms. However, the Manx Longhair (called Cymric [pronounced *kim-rick*] by some associations) is not recognised by all cat registries. The potential colour and pattern range in the breed is extremely extensive.

All patterns and colours are acceptable in some associations but, at this time, most registries do not recognise the Siamese Pattern. This is called Colourpoint when applied to other breeds. The numerically small number of Manx breeders means that many of the theoretically available patterns and colours may be extremely difficult, if not impossible, to find.

DEFINING A BREED
A breed enjoys status as such if one or more feline registries have granted it recognition for exhibition purposes. This can only be done after a specialist, or a number of them, have drafted a standard of points against which all cats of that breed can be compared. The standard is thus an official blueprint of a breed, and is presented to a registration body for their adoption. If it meets their criteria (these differ between associations), the breed will be granted recognition. The standard will then be used by judges in all shows under that registry's rules.

The standard of points provides a description of a theoretically ideal example, but such that it also has flexibility that takes account of the fact that no two cats are ever quite the same. To achieve these dual objectives, a standard can never be a precise document. As a consequence, many of the terms used in it are relative and open to considerable interpretation, by both judges and breeders.

While the standards of various feline registries are broadly similar, they may differ in their extent and in what is and is not acceptable within their associa-

Similar in many respects to the British Shorthair, the Manx possesses a large and fairly round head, with large round eyes.

tion. This extends to both the colours and patterns. Examples of the breed seen in colours or patterns not standardised must be exhibited in classes called Any Other Colour (AOC). In terms of bodily parts, as in the tailed varieties of the Manx, any variants are exhibited in Any Other Variety (AOV) classes.

Apart from a written description of a breed, a standard also lists any faults that are especially appropriate to it, as opposed to faults applicable to any breed. General faults are listed separately by an association in their list of withholding or disqualification faults applicable to all breeds.

ALLOCATION OF POINTS
The standard allocates a total of 100 points to a cat. These points are spread across various features. These are normally the head, ears, eyes, body, legs, feet, coat and colour pattern. In the case of the anatomical mutational breeds, points are also allocated to the mutation. In the Manx this is taillessness. The various feline associations invariably differ on the number of the points this is given.

In the standard of the GCCF of Britain, the lack of tail accounts for 25 points, whereas in the CFA of America only 5 points are given. The points, as opposed to the written description, indicate the importance a registry gives to

the varying aspects of that breed. This has both positive and negative potential. On the one hand, it underscores the value of certain features to the breed but, conversely, this can be the source of potential neglect.

If a feature has a high allocation of points, breeders will tend to focus on that feature. Such focus may become excessive to the point that the feature becomes unduly altered. This is why certain breeds have changed over the years, the Persian and the Siamese being the most obvious examples.

Interpreting a standard requires considerable skill, which takes years to acquire. Even then, not everyone will agree that a given breeder or judge has applied the standard correctly. The points are, of course, a necessity for judging. The judge will deduct points where deemed appropriate. The cat with the least number of deductions will be the class winner.

The first Manx standard was drafted by Harrison Weir in 1889 and has changed somewhat over the years, as has the number of points allocated to certain

features. In his original standard, Weir spread the points across seven features. This rose to ten by the 1960s, but is now down to five.

The following breed description is not that of any one association. It has been prepared after comparing those of three major feline registries. These are the Governing Council of the Cat Fancy (GCCF) of Britain, and the Cat Fanciers Association (CFA) and The International Cat Association (TICA), both of America. That of the CFA is the most detailed.

The description should meet the needs of most owners. A few additional comments have been integrated to provide a better understanding of the standard. Those who plan to breed or exhibit should obtain the standard of the association with which their cats are to be registered.

BREED DESCRIPTION

HEAD
The head should be of medium to large size and round (fairly round in the GCCF). The cheeks should be prominent and the muzzle well developed. The nose is of medium length, broad and straight. It should display a very gentle curve where it meets the forehead, with no obvious stop or indentation. The whisker pads are prominent. In profile the head is of medium

Manx breeders strive to produce kittens that will adhere to the standard as adults. Whether you are purchasing a pet cat or a show cat, you still want a cat that is healthy and typical of the Manx breed.

length. A level bite is required, meaning that the upper incisors should just touch those of the lower jaw. The neck should be short and thick.

EYES

Large and round, the eyes should be set such that they show just a slight inclination towards the nose. Their colour should preferably be in keeping with the coat colour.

EARS

Medium to somewhat tall, the ears should display a slight outward inclination. The base is well open and the ears taper to a rounded tip. The ear furnishings—the hairs emanating from the base of the ear—are sparse in the Manx, but full in the Manx Longhair.

BODY

Of cobby build, the Manx is a well-muscled breed displaying a good width of chest. The back is short in length and displays a gentle arc from the shoulders to the higher rump. The flank—the area between the ribs and the hip—is especially deep in this breed.

LEGS AND PAWS

The front legs are short in comparison with those of the hindquarters. They are of ample bone, well muscled, and set well apart to emphasise the broad, deep chest.

The hind legs are long and have powerful deep thighs. The height of the hindquarters should be approximately equal to the back's length.

The paws are round and neat. They have five toes on the front paws, one of which is the dew claw, and four on the hind paws. When viewed from the front, or from the rear, the legs should be straight.

TAILLESSNESS

The standard of the GCCF differs slightly from that of American standards in respect of this feature. The GCCF requires that absolute taillessness is essential, whereas the CFA and TICA use the words 'appears to be tailless.' The GCCF states that no definite rise of bone or cartilage should be felt, which would interfere with the roundness of the rump. Very often there is a slight dimple where the first caudal vertebra would normally be found.

The American standards are somewhat more relaxed on this matter. They state that a rise of bone or cartilage should not be penalised as long as this does not stop the hand of a judge and spoil the roundness of the rump as a consequence. The completely tailless Manx is called a 'Rumpy.' Any other form is regarded as being a Manx variant for breeding and registration purposes.

The cat's body consists of thousands of muscles, comprising a complex system that allows the domestic cat to be among the most flexible animals in the world.

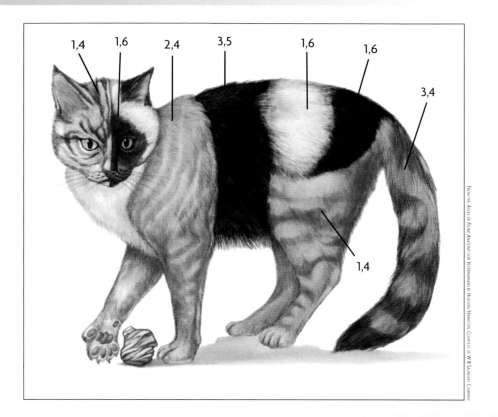

1,4   1,6   2,4   3,5   1,6   1,6   3,4   1,4

PARTICOLOURED CAT

Not a new breed of feline, this 'particoloured cat' illustrates the many possibilities of the feline coat. Since cats come in three basic hair lengths, short, long and rex (curly), all three coat lengths are illustrated here. Additionally, different coat patterns, such as mackerel tabby, Abyssinian and self-coloured, are depicted to demonstrate the differences.

1–3   COAT TYPES
  1 Shorthair coat
  2 Rex (curly) coat
  3 Longhair coat

4–6   COAT COLOUR PATTERNS
  4 Mackerel (tabby)
  5 Abyssinian
  6 Self-coloured

SKIN AND HAIRCOAT OF CATS

Schematic illustration of histologic layers of the integument skin.

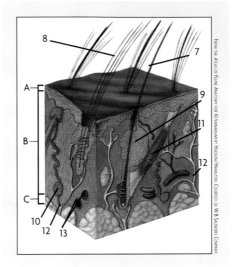

A Epidermis
B Dermis
C Subcutis

7 Primary hair
8 Secondary hairs
9 Area of sebaceous gland
10 Apocrine sweat gland
11 M arrector pili
12 Nerve fibre
13 Cutaneous vessels
14 Tactile hair
15 Fibrous capsule
16 Venous sinus
17 Sensory nerve fibres
18 External root sheath
19 Hair papilla

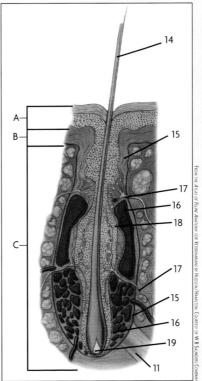

Schematic illustration of a tactile hair (whisker).

FROM THE ATLAS OF FELINE ANATOMY FOR VETERINARIANS BY HUDSON/HAMILTON. COURTESY OF W B SAUNDERS COMPANY.

FROM THE ATLAS OF FELINE ANATOMY FOR VETERINARIANS BY HUDSON/HAMILTON. COURTESY OF W B SAUNDERS COMPANY.

COAT

This is short but dense. It is described as being a double coat. This means that a thick soft undercoat is overlaid by guard hairs that are slightly longer, coarser and glossy. The two coats combine to create an excellent all-weather coat that protects from both cold and wet weather. During the warmer months, the coat will be less dense as some of the fur, the undercoat in particular, is shed.

The quality of the coat is always of much greater importance than its colour or pattern, which are allocated no points in Britain and only 5 by CFA and TICA. GCCF judges only consider the colour and pattern if all other aspects of the cats under assessment are equal.

COAT (LONGHAIR)

As with the Manx Shorthair, the Longhair coat is double, featuring a dense undercoat. The topcoat is soft, silky and of medium length. It shows gradual increase in length from the shoulder to the rump. This can make the body look longer than that of the Manx Shorthair. The hair on the breeches, abdomen and neck-ruff is usually longer than that on the main part of the body. Toe and ear tufts are desirable.

BREED FAULTS

The following are the faults listed by the various associations, which

COAT PATTERNS

Agouti	Pigments band the hair, named after the rodent that possesses this pattern.
Non-agouti	Coat colour exhibits a self colour or carries two or more colours.
Shell	Darker colour on tips of the hair; lower portion lighter in colour.
Shaded	Darker colour extends further down the hair than in the shell.
Bicolour	Solid colour with white pattern.

are subject to either disqualification or penalty:

- Definite rise of bone or cartilage at the end of the spine such that it interferes with the roundness of the rump. An uneven dental bite. Weak chin (usually the result of an incorrect bite). Incorrect number of toes (usually having more than stipulated). Any evidence of weakness in the hindquarters, such as an inability to stand or walk correctly. Level back. Rangy body. Hind legs too short. Lack of adequate bone structure. Bowed or cowhocked hind legs. Incorrect eye set, meaning too straight or too Oriental. Lack of

MANX SELF-COLOURS

COLOUR	DESCRIPTION
White	Pure and untainted with yellow. Eye colour may be blue, orange or odd-eyed, meaning one in each colour. Nose leather and paw pads pink. White is associated with either unilateral or bilateral deafness. This is more likely to be evident if the eye colour is blue, though only marginally so. White is the result of a dominant mutation that prevents colour pigment from forming. If white is combined with a colour, as in the bicoloured cats, for example, there are no associated hearing problems.
Black	A dense, coal black. Eye colour copper-orange. Nose leather and paw pads black, though the pads may also be a dark brown. A recessive mutation creates the colour by allowing dark pigment to replace the orange pigment seen in the ground colour of the tabby pattern.
Blue	More of a slate blue-grey or smoke blue. Eye colour is copper-orange. Nose leather and paw pads blue. The colour is created by a recessive mutation that causes the black pigment to coalesce into globules. The clear space between these reflects light and gives the visual impression that the black has been diluted. Dilute is the commonly used name for the gene at the density gene locus, even though the pigment has not actually been diluted.
Chocolate	This colour is only accepted if the Colourpoint pattern is accepted, the pattern from which it was originally derived. It can be any shade of rich chocolate. Eye colour copper-orange. Nose leather and paw pads chocolate or pink. The colour is created by a recessive mutation that degrades black pigment to brown.
Lilac (Lavender)	A greyish colour with pinkish tones. It is also known in America as frost. Eye colour copper-orange. Nose leather and paw pads pinkish-lilac. The dilution gene acting on chocolate creates the colour.
Red	A brilliant deep rich red, not the orange of the typical ginger moggie cat. Eye colour copper-orange. Nose leather and paw pads brick red. This colour is unusual in that it is linked to the sex chromosomes. It is the gene that enables the tortoiseshell pattern to be created and is a dominant mutation.
Cream	A colour that is neither an obvious pale red nor a fawn. Described by CFA as 'one level shade of buff cream without markings.' Eye colour copper-orange. Nose leather and paw pads brick red. This colour is the dilution of red, so is sex-linked. The richness of red, on which the dilution mutation is working, will determine its shade.

a double coat. Coat of one overall length in the Manx Longhair.

COAT COLOURS AND PATTERNS

The potential list of coat colours and patterns is bewildering because these can be combined in many ways. For example, the patterns may have more than one variety—in the tabby, there are four types. Each of these can be seen in the various colours. The tabby can be combined with the tortoiseshell to create the tortie-tabby or torbie, as it is also known. This can then be seen in the various colours. The colours can also be combined with white.

SELF-COLOURS

A self-colour is one that is the same all over the cat's body. Ideally it should be free of any shading, meaning different tones of the same colour, these usually being darker on the back. The colour should be solid to the roots. Normally, lockets of white appearing on a self-colour would be penalised in most breeds. However, this is not so in the Manx. Indeed, in 1979 a black Manx (Grand Champion Tatleberry Long John) with a white chest

MANX CAT TABBY VARIETIES

COLOUR	DESCRIPTION
Mackerel Tabby	This is the original tabby developed from the wild ancestors of the domestic cat. It comprises vertical stripes that extend from a lateral line that runs parallel with the spinal stripe. It is commonly known in America as the tiger pattern. The more vertical stripes, the better.
Classic or Blotched Tabby	This is more popular with exhibitors than the Mackerel because it is more eye-catching. A central oyster-shaped blotch on each flank is surrounded by one or more complete circles.
Spotted Tabby	In this variety, round, oval or rosette-shaped markings cover the body. Their distribution in the coat will follow one of the two other tabby patterns, as though these patterns have broken up into small blotches.
Ticked Tabby	This pattern is rarely seen as a pattern of a breed. It is best known for its being the basis of the Abyssinian and Singapura breeds. The pattern is genetically known as agouti. It comprises hairs banded with two or more darker pigments. The lie of the coat creates the ticked effect.

MANX COLOURPOINT

SOLID POINT COLOURS

POINT COLOUR	BODY COLOUR
SEAL BROWN	Beige shading to creamy white.
BLUE	Bluish white shading to white.
CHOCOLATE	Ivory shading to white.
LILAC	Magnolia white shading to white.
RED	Apricot shading to white.
CREAM	Lighter cream shading to white.

TORTIE POINT COLOURS

POINT COLOUR	BODY COLOUR
SEAL BROKEN WITH SHADES OF RED	Toning creamy body colour.
BLUE-CREAM BLUE BROKEN WITH SHADES OF CREAM	Glacial to creamy white.
CHOCOLATE BROKEN WITH SHADES OF RED	Ivory to apricot white.
LILAC-CREAM LILAC BROKEN WITH SHADES OF CREAM	Magnolia to creamy.

TABBY POINT COLOURS

Tabby is restricted to the points. The colours are seal, blue, chocolate, lilac, red and cream.

TORTIE TABBY POINT COLOURS

Both the tortie and the tabby elements must be present though the extent and distribution of these is not important. The colours are seal, blue-cream, chocolate and lilac-cream.

locket was the adult winner of the GCCF's major annual show—The Supreme. The self-colours for the Manx are: white, black, blue, chocolate, lilac, red and cream.

COAT PATTERNS

Tabby: There are four varieties of the tabby pattern—mackerel, classic, spotted and ticked—but only three are normally seen as pattern varieties within breeds. The varieties are distinguished by their body pattern, with the facial, leg, chest, abdomen, and tail markings being similar in each variety.

Such markings are an 'M' on the forehead, necklets across the chest, bands across the legs, rings on the tail and a dorsal stripe that goes from the neck to the tail. The eye colour in tabbies is copper-orange other than in the silver variety in which it is green or blue-green.

The tortoiseshell pattern shows two colours at the same time. In America if the colours should form distinct areas, they are called patched. The familiar contraction of the term tortoise-shell is the word 'tortie'.

Tipped: There are three tipped varieties—tipped, shaded and smoke—each being named for the extent of tipping. The non-pigmented part of the hair is so pale as to appear white. If the colour pigment is restricted to only the very tip of each hair, this is called tipped or chinchilla. In the black-tipped (silver chinchiila), the eye colour is green or blue-green, but in all other colours it is copper-orange. In the shaded pattern, the pigment extends down to about one-third of the hair's length. It is, therefore, a darker pattern than the chinchilla. In the smoke variation, the pigment extends about two-thirds down the hair shaft. The result is that the coat appears to be a self-colour until the cat moves, when the white undercoat becomes evident. This creates a pattern of changing appearance. Eye colour is copper-orange, including the black smoke.

Bi-Colour: In this pattern, one colour is combined with white. The white is normally preferred to be on the face, chest, legs and underparts, but this is not a requirement of the standard. If the colour is restricted to the head, legs and tail, this is called the Van pattern, after the Turkish Van breed. One or two small blotches of body colour are acceptable on the Van.

Tortoiseshell: This famous pattern is unusual in that two colours are seen in the coat at the same time. It is derived from the sex-linked red. In Britain and many other countries, the two colours can be randomly scattered in the coat as long as each is clearly visible.

In America, it is preferred that the colours form distinct patches—thus giving rise to the term *patched* when combined with the tabby pattern.

In Britain, the tortoiseshell is also known as the tortie. When combined with the tabby pattern, this creates the tortie-tabby, also called the torbie. When the tortie is combined with white, the result is the attractive tortie and white, known as calico in America and some other countries.

The pattern is created by a colour—black, blue, chocolate or lilac—being able to manifest itself in part of the coat, but not in others. In these other areas, the coat is shades of red, or of cream if the base colour is a dilution as with the blue or the lilac. The blue tortie is more commonly called the blue-cream. The tortie pattern is normally a female-only variety. Males are produced on occasions though most, but not all, are infertile.

Colourpoint: Once unique to the Siamese breed, this pattern has been transferred to many breeds under the name of Colourpoint or, more rarely, Himalayan. The mask, ears, legs, and tail are of a darker colour than the rest of the body. The pattern is created by a mutation that is heat-sensitive.

Normal colour pigment forms only on the coolest parts of the body, which are the extremities. The rest of the coat is warmer, so pigment density is restricted, creating a paler shade of the given colour. However, even at the extremities the pigment is reduced to a very dark brown called seal.

SHADED COLOURS

COLOUR	DESCRIPTION	EYE COLOUR
SILVER	White with black tipping.	Emerald or blue-green.
GOLDEN	Apricot undercoat becoming golden at the tip.	Emerald or blue-green.
RED-SHADED CAMEO	White evenly shaded with red.	Orange-copper.
CREAM-SHADED CAMEO	White evenly shaded with cream.	Orange-copper.
PEWTER	Similiar to silver but a little darker.	Orange-copper.

MANX CAT

Before the decision to purchase a Manx is made, careful consideration should be given to the breed itself and to the responsibilities of cat ownership. If more owners would do this, there would be far fewer half-starved pets roaming our streets or having to live in local animal rescue centres.

OWNER RESPONSIBILITY

The initial cost of a Manx represents only a fraction of its lifetime's cost. The first question is, 'Can you afford one?' The kitten needs vaccinations to protect it against various diseases. Boosters are then required every year. Cat food is more costly than that for dogs. There is also the cost of cat litter every week. Periodic vet checks and treatment for illness or accident must be allowed for. When holidays are taken, you may need to board the pet at a cattery.

From the outset, there will be additional costs apart from that of the kitten. It will need a basket, carrying box, feeding bowls and grooming utensils, scratching post and maybe a collar and a few toys. If you have any doubts at all about

THE PURCHASING PROCESS

Never rush into the purchase of a companion that is to be given the freedom of your home and will become an integral part of your life. A pure-bred cat may live 20 or more years. This is a long time. It is very prudent to take all those steps that will minimise the chances of your ever regretting the choice you make. Once you have decided on the sex, age, reason for purchase (pet, show or breeding) and desired colour pattern, proceed cautiously, heeding all the advice given here. By following a planned process of selection, you will also gain much useful information.

being able to supply all these needs, it is best not to obtain a cat.

Other matters also need careful thought. If you are planning to have a family, will your love for the Manx be compromised once a baby arrives? Cats are generally not a problem with family newcomers, providing they are not ignored or treated as a threat to the baby. Never purchase a kitten for a child unless you want one yourself. If you are elderly, it is only fair to consider what would happen to your cherished pet if it were to outlive you or if you were to become hospitalised for long periods.

It is most unfortunate that many people rush into the purchase of cats on impulse. They then find they cannot cope if problems, and extra costs, ensue. Some lose interest in the pet once it matures past its kitten stage. The evidence of these realities is easily seen in the growing number of cats abandoned or taken to animal shelters every year. Invariably their owners will make feeble excuses for why the cat cannot be kept. But the bottom line is they did not stop to consider at the outset what responsible ownership entailed.

If you are looking for an all-action breed, or its opposite, the Manx is not the best choice. But if you want a confiding pet that will

DOCUMENTATION

When you take delivery of your kitten, certain paperwork should come with it:

1. Three- to five-generation pedigree.
2. Breeder-signed registration application form or change of owner registration form. This assumes the breeder has registered stock. If they have not, the kitten cannot be registered at a later date. It is worth less than the kitten with registration paperwork. You are not recommended to purchase a kitten from unregistered parents.
3. Certificates of health, vaccination and neutering, if this has been effected. Ideally, it is desirable that the kitten's parents have been tested negative for major diseases. Additionally, the breeder should know the blood group of your kitten. This may be of importance at a later date.
4. Details of worming or other treatments attended.
5. Diet sheet, feeding timetable and brand names of food items used. This diet should be maintained for at least ten days while the kitten adjusts to the trauma of moving home.
6. Signed receipt for monies paid.
7. Signed copy of any guarantees. Not all breeders give a guarantee on the reasonable grounds that once the kitten leaves their care, its onward well-being is no longer under their control.

have more than a few moments of mischief, without actually becoming a delinquent, the Manx would likely prove very suitable.

In a quiet home with no children or other pets, a Manx will tend to be quiet itself. In a full family situation, it will tend to get involved in more activities. The more involved it gets, the more its unique individual personality will develop.

The Manx is a quiet breed not prone to neurotic behaviour. Its small gene pool is, and is likely to remain, very stable in desirable areas, such as being bold (outgoing) and friendly, as well as able to interact extremely well with most people and other pets.

KITTEN OR ADULT?

Most potential owners normally want a kitten because it is so cute, cuddly and playful. A kitten is easily trained and has not yet developed bad habits, which the older Manx may have done. This said, if you plan to breed or exhibit, there are advantages in obtaining a young adult. Other potential owners, such as the elderly, may benefit by avoiding the demanding needs of a young kitten. In both these instances, a good age is when the youngster is 9–15 months old. Even a fully mature Manx may prove an excellent choice for some owners.

Manx kittens should not be obtained until four months old.

No reputable breeder will sell them younger than this, so do not purchase a Manx kitten under four months old. The reason is that any negative effects due to the Manx mutation usually arise between birth and four months of age. If a kitten is healthy at four months old, there is much less risk of problems developing as it grows older.

SEX & COLOUR PATTERN

If it is to be purely a pet, the Manx's gender is unimportant. Both are delightful. Males are usually larger, bolder and more outgoing. Females tend to be more discerning about which humans they like. However, each Manx is an individual. Its character and health, more than its sex, should

TAKING KITTY HOME

Arrange collection of the kitten as early in the day as possible. If a long journey is involved, be sure to take a few breaks so kitty does not suffer from travel sickness. Do not make stops to show the kitten to friends; this represents a health hazard. Once home, offer the kitten a drink, then allow it to sleep if it so requires. Children must be educated to handle a kitten gently, to never tease it and to respect its sleeping privacy. Until it is litter-trained, it should be restricted to the kitchen or another room with an easy-to-clean floor surface.

The irresistibility of a Manx kitten is ineffable! Acquiring a kitten is an exciting experience, though you should never disregard the responsibilities that accompany the commitment of cat ownership.

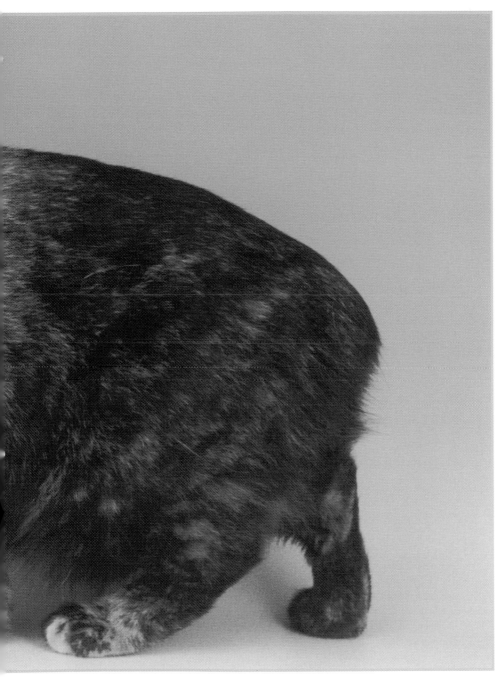

A Best in Show winner, Grand International Premier and European Ch Jindivik Ballawhane is a tortie Manx, owned by Kristiina Rautio and Juhani Kurki.

be the basis of selection. Again, the sex is unimportant for the potential exhibitor. It is not even necessary for the cat to be sexually 'entire.' Classes for neuters are featured in shows.

Those with breeding aspirations are advised to obtain only females. All pet owners should regard neutering (males) and spaying (females) as obligatory. Today this can be effected at any age after eight weeks.

The colour pattern is a matter of personal preference. It should never be placed ahead of health and character. Some colours and patterns will be more readily available than others. The more popular varieties may be less costly than the rarer ones. This would generally not apply to prospective breeding or exhibition individuals, where type quality will be as important as colour or pattern.

LOOK BEFORE YOU LEAP
It is important you meet as many Manx breeders and kittens as you can. This gives you a good mental picture of what an healthy typical example should look like and cost for the quality and colour you want. Normally, you will get what you pay for. If you look for the cheapest kitten, there will be a sound reason why it is the cheapest!

The best place to start your search is a cat show. At large cat shows, most of the colour varieties will be on display. Purchase the show catalogue. It lists all the exhibitors and their addresses. You can see if any live in your immediate locality. Whenever possible, it is best to purchase locally so you can visit the home of the breeder. Some breeders will insist you do so in order to be satisfied that you will make a good owner.

Shows and breeders are advertised in the various cat magazines available from news agents. You can also contact a major cat registry, which will supply a list of national and regional clubs, which in turn are able to supply breeder lists. When visiting a breeder, always make an appointment. Try to visit no more than one cattery a day. This reduces the risk that you may transport pathogens (disease-causing organisms) from one establishment to the next. Selecting a good breeder is a case of noting the environment in which the cats are kept, the attitude of the owner to you and their cats, and how friendly and healthy the kittens look. It is vital the chosen kitty has an outgoing personality. It must not appear timid or very shy. This indicates a lack of breeder socialisation or a genetic weakness in its temperament. Either way, it is not a kitten you should select.

CHOOSING A KITTEN

If you choose the breeder wisely, and especially if a friend recommends him, this should remove all problems related to your making a poor choice. However, a little knowledge on what to look for will not go amiss. Observe the kittens from a distance to ensure none is unduly lethargic, which is never a good sign. If any kitten displays signs of illness, this should bring to an end any further thoughts of purchase from that source. A reputable breeder would not allow a sickly kitten to remain within his litter.

It is always advisable to select a kitten that shows partic-ular interest in you. Manx are very discerning. If both of you are drawn to each other, this will greatly enhance the bonding essential for a strong relation-ship.

Once a particular kitten has been selected, it should be given a close physical inspection. The eyes and nose must show no signs of weeping or discharge. The ears will be erect and fresh smelling. The coat should look healthy, never dry and dull. There must be no signs of parasites in the fur. There will be no bald areas of fur, nor bodily swellings or abrasions. Inspect the anal region. This must be clean with no indication of congealed faecal matter. Any

AN HEALTHY KITTEN

Closely inspect any kitten before making a final decision. Keep in mind the following points:

Eyes and nose: Clean and clear with no signs of discharge.

Ears: Fresh-smelling and erect.

Coat: Healthy, not dull or dry.

Anal region: Clean with no staining of the fur.

Feet: Four toes on each foot, plus a dewclaw on the inside of each front leg.

Teeth: Correct bite.

There should be no signs of parasites or bald areas of fur. A potbelly may indicate worms.

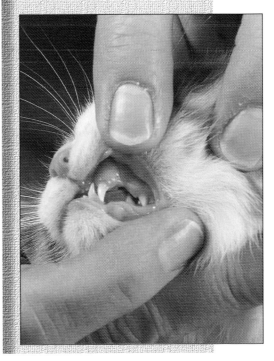

ADOPTING AN ADULT

Some owners, such as the elderly, may benefit by adopting an adult cat. They can avoid the demanding needs of a young kitten and enjoy the advantages of a well-trained adult, making grooming an easier task. Breeders and exhibitors can also benefit from purchasing an older cat because it is easier to assess the quality. Sometimes, though, older cats can have bad habits that are hard to break. So if you are thinking about obtaining an older cat, it is important to thoroughly investigate possible behavioural and health problems

develop at the same rate. Minor imperfections may correct themselves (they may also get worse), but major faults will not. Inspect the feet to see there are four toes on each, plus a dewclaw on the inside of each front leg.

With respect to the colour, there is no link between this and health other than deafness in certain white varieties. Any faults in the colour or its placement will only be of importance in breeding or exhibition individuals. The potential breeder/exhibitor should obtain a copy of the official standard so he is *au fait* with all colour, pattern and bodily faults of the breed.

KITTY SHOPPING SPREE

Certain accessories should be regarded as obligatory and obtained before the kitten arrives at your home.

SCRATCHING POST

This will save the furniture from being abused! There are many models, some being simple posts, others are combined with play stations and sleeping quarters, which are the best.

LITTER BOX(ES)

Some are open trays; others are domed to provide extra privacy. Still others have special bases in which odour removers are fitted.

staining of the fur indicates current or recent diarrhoea.

The kitten must not display a potbelly. This may indicate worms or other internal disorders. Check the teeth to be sure of a correct bite. Bear in mind that the jawbones do not

Grooming tools are among the supplies you will need to purchase for your new Manx.

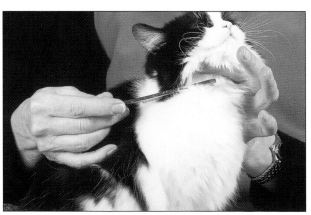

Purchase a top-quality scratching post for your Manx cat. The posts that are combined with play stations are preferred by active Manx cats and their owners.

Your local pet shop should carry a full range of litter trays, litter boxes and the tools with which you keep the box clean.

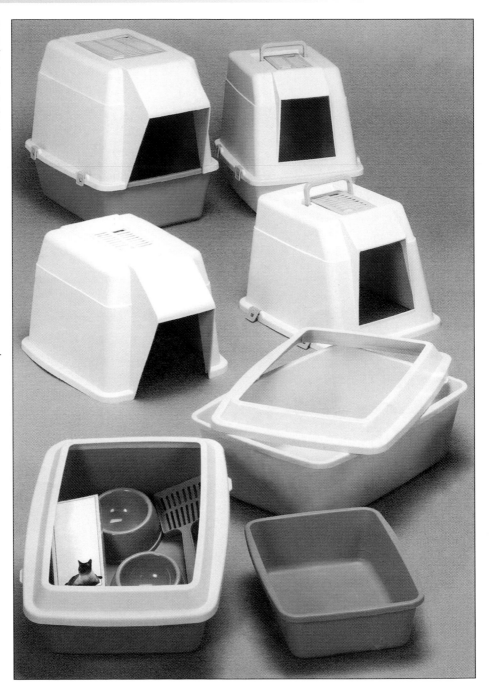

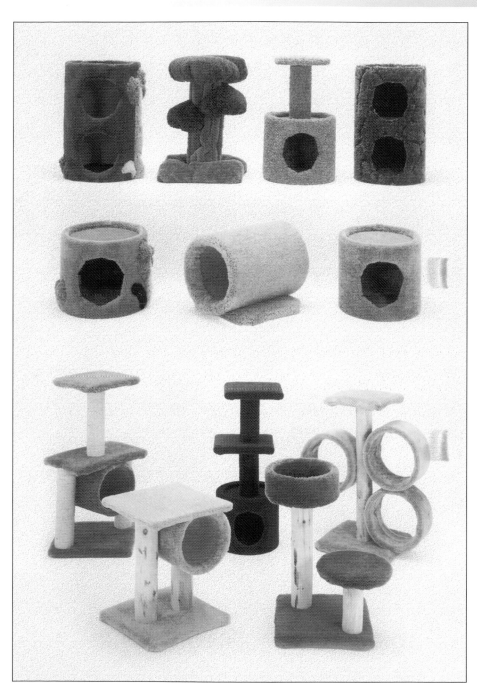

Your local pet shop should have an array of scratching posts that will delight your Manx. Do not attempt to make a post yourself as many carpets are too weak to stand the tearing or may have been dyed with chemicals harmful to cats.

Cat toys are entertaining for cat and owner alike. Purchase toys that require interaction between you and your Manx, thereby affording the cat exercise and companionship while playing.

Cat carriers are a necessity of cat ownership, though no cat welcomes the opportunity of being carted about in a crate. Nonetheless, the carrier is the only safe option for transport to the veterinary surgeon.

Double-bowl feeders are very convenient for feeding your cat. Go to your pet shop to purchase top-quality feeders, which should come in a variety of colours, styles and sizes.

There is nothing glamorous about purchasing a litter box, yet cat owners have few options in this regard. Visit your local pet shop to see a selection of boxes. Some cats do not accept a covered box, while others welcome the 'privacy.'

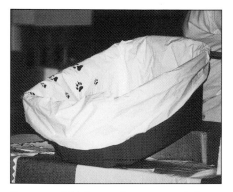

Liners are available for most litter trays to assist in keeping them clean and more manageable.

Purchasing a scratching post is a smart option for the cat owner. It's best to purchase a sturdy, well-made post that will last your cat years of utility.

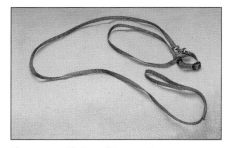

If you are considering walking your Manx, you must have a lead that is suitable for a cat.

HOMEMADE TOYS

Cats love to play and pet shops have many cat toys to choose from. Sometimes, however, people give their cats homemade toys. These can be harmful to your cat, as they could have pieces that could break off and be swallowed. Only give your pet toys from the pet shop that have been proven safe for cats.

CAT LITTER
There are numerous types on the market, each offering advantages and drawbacks. Avoid the low-cost types that contain a lot of dangerous dust. Use those that are fully biodegradable.

FOOD/WATER DISHES
Polished metal has the longest-wear life. Earthenware is less costly than metal and superior to the plastic types.

GROOMING TOOLS
These will comprise a good-quality bristle brush, a fine-toothed comb, nail trimmers and a soft chamois leather.

CAT COLLAR AND/OR HARNESS
Select elasticised collars. Be sure a name and address disc or barrel is fitted to this. A harness must be a snug but comfortable fit if it is to be effective.

THE LAP CAT
The coat of the Manx may be long or short: both of these affect its potential as a lap cat. The Shorthaired Manx, as in other aspects, will prove to be a middle-of-the-road breed regarding its lap cat potential. The Longhair will be less suitable. The reason for saying these things is because heat gain or loss is crucial in lap potential. The Manx has an excellent weatherproof coat. This means it can get uncomfortably hot in a relatively short period of time when lying on its owner's warm lap, especially during the warmer months.

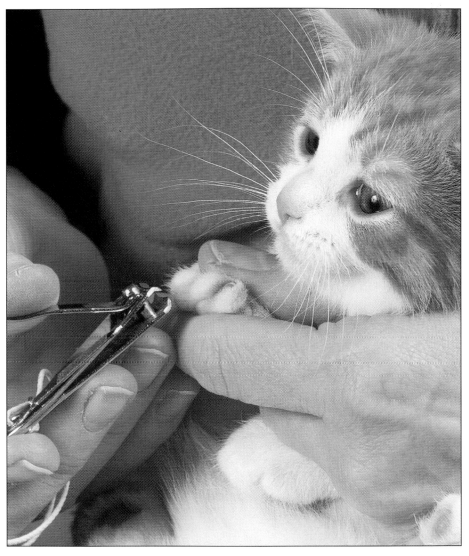

Start clipping your Manx kitten's nails regularly. It's much easier to trim a cat's nails if it is accustomed to the procedure when young.

CARRYING BOX
This is essential for transporting the cat to the vet or other places, as well as for home restriction when needed. Be sure it is large enough to accommodate a fully-grown Manx, not just a kitten. The choice is between collapsible models, soft plastic types and, the best choice, those made of wood or fibreglass.

MANX CAT

For a kitten, its human environment holds many dangers. Its owner must protect it from these until it becomes agile and wiser. The following dangers lurk in typical households. Always check whether there are additional ones in your home. The most important decision you need to make from the outset is whether or not the kitten is to be given outdoor liberty.

HOW MUCH FREEDOM?

More than at any time in the past the question of how much freedom a cat should be given is the subject of heated debate. It is a very subjective matter. Here the more pertinent points are given so you can relate these to your home location. This, to a very large degree, should influence your decision.

Cats living in or close to an urban area are at the highest safety risk. The amount of traffic is such that death from road accidents is a major concern. In such environments there are high dog populations, some of which are feral or vicious. Injury or death from dog attacks is therefore another major source of danger to a feline.

Urban cat populations are also extremely high. Far too many cats are living a virtually feral existence. These are tough, streetwise cats that often carry fleas and other parasites that are vectors of disease. Some will be carriers of, or infected with, feline leukaemia and other deadly diseases.

The typical feline family pet can be badly injured if it becomes engaged in fights with these roaming bullies. Furthermore, their very presence in and around a gentle cat's garden can cause the pet severe stress. This can make it fearful of stepping outside its

BE ONE JUMP AHEAD

Seemingly innocuous things, such as doors, can become life-threatening should they suddenly slam shut on a kitten due to a strong draught. When windows and external doors are open, be sure internal doors are secured with a doorstop. At all times be one jump ahead of a kitten in terms of identifying dangerous situations.

home. In some instances, it may cause the pet to actually leave its home.

Sadly, as if these risks are not enough, there is no shortage of people who will steal a pedigreed cat, the more so if it is friendly. Add to this the number of abusive people who do not like cats roaming into their gardens, and the scenario is not good. Finally, free-roaming cats also take a heavy toll on local bird and wildlife populations.

Taking these various facts into account, the urban cat is best kept indoors. It can enjoy the benefit of the outdoors if supplied with a roomy aviary-type exercise pen. Some cats can be trained to walk on a lead. This allows outdoor enjoyment, even if this is restricted to the garden. When walking your cat in public places, use only a harness. This is much

THE TRAVELLING CAT

Whenever your cat needs to be taken on a car journey, never let it travel loose in the vehicle, which is illegal. It must always be in its carrying box. If a cat were to go under the clutch or brake pedal when the car was moving, this would be dangerous to all occupants. A cat might also spring from one seat to another, which might distract the driver. This could have disastrous results.

Never leave a cat alone in a car on a hot day. The temperature can rise dramatically to the point that the cat is unable to breathe. It could die of heat stroke. Always leave a window partially open, but not so wide that the agile cat could escape.

DANGEROUS DISINFECTANTS

Although owners should disinfect the litter box regularly to prevent disease and illness, some household disinfectants can be harmful to cats. Pine-oil-based cleaners are toxic to cats. DO NOT use them. Products containing Phenol should also be avoided. Bleach is a good disinfectant to use; however, be sure to rinse the litter box thoroughly and air it out to get rid of any fumes.

safer than a collar.

In contrast to urban situations, the cat living in a rural environment is far safer, the more so if there are no immediate neighbours or busy roads. Even so, it is wise to restrict the cat's outdoor freedom to daylight hours. During the night it is more likely to get run over or to threaten local wildlife.

Those living between the extremes of isolated areas and busy urban environments should consider the local risk factor. Generally it is best to keep the cat indoors but to provide an outdoor exercise pen.

An exercise pen is
the best outdoor
option for Manx
of all ages.

An exercise pen is the best outdoor option for Manx of all ages.

HOUSEHOLD DANGERS

Within its home, a kitten is best viewed as an accident waiting to happen! The most dangerous room is the kitchen. Hot electric hobs, naked flames from gas rings, boiling pans of food or water, and sinks full of water are obvious hazards. An iron left on its board with cable trailing to the floor is an invitation to a kitten to jump up—with potentially fatal consequences. Washing machines or spin dryers with warm clothes in them, and their doors open, are inviting places to nap. Always check the kitty isn't inside if the door has been left open. Cupboards containing poisonous or other dangerous substances should always be kept securely closed.

In the living room, the normal dangers are aquariums without hoods, unguarded fires, electric bar heaters, poisonous indoor plants, trailing electrical wires and ornaments that may be knocked over by a mischievous kitty. Toilets can be fatal to an over-curious kitten. The same is true of a bath containing water. Balconies should be safeguarded to remove the potential for the kitten to slip and fall.

OTHER DANGERS

Other potential dangers are when electric tools are left lying about and connected to power outlets— even worse if they are left on, as with bench saws. If the kitten is given freedom to exercise in a garden containing a pond, the kitten must be under constant supervision. Cherished ornaments should be placed out of reach of the kitten, as much for their safety as to any danger they may present to the kitty. It's not always the direct danger of something that can be the problem. If an ornament or similar item crashes to the floor, this can startle the kitten into a panicked departure! The kitten could then fall from a shelf in its haste.

THE GARAGE AND SHED

These two buildings are very dangerous to a kitten. Sharp and heavy tools, nails, glass jars, garden weed killers and open tins of paint are but a sampling of the items the average family uses or stores in these. A kitten may clamber into the engine compartment of a vehicle. This could be fatal if the owner happened to start the engine before the kitten had removed itself. Always know where the kitten is.

MANX CAT

Today the feeding of cats has been reduced to its most simple level with the availability of many scientifically prepared commercial diets. However, this fact can result in owners' becoming casual in their approach to the subject. While the main object of a given diet is to provide the ingredients that promote healthy growth and maximum immunity to disease, it also fulfils an important secondary role.

A proper diet must maintain in the cat a psychological feeling of well-being that avoids nutritionally-related stress problems or syndromes. By ensuring the diet is balanced, of good variety, and never monotonous, these dual roles will be achieved. This approach will also avoid the situation of the cat's becoming a finicky eater.

BALANCE AND VARIETY

A balanced diet means one that contains all of the major ingredients—protein, fats, carbohydrates, vitamins and minerals—in the ratios needed to ensure maximum growth and health. Variety means supplying foods in a range of forms that will maintain and stimulate the cat's interest in its meals. Commercially formulated foods come in three levels of moisture: low (dried), semi-moist and moist (tinned).

Generally, the dried and moist forms are the most popular. Dried cat foods have the advantage that they can be left in the cat dish for longer periods of time than tinned foods. They are ideal for supplying on a free-choice basis. Like the tinned varieties, they come in a wide range of popular flavours.

In order to meet the specific needs of a kitten, there are specially formulated foods available. These contain the higher protein levels needed by a growing kitten. As it grows, the

MILK AND CATS

Milk, although associated with cats, is not needed once kittenhood has passed. Indeed, excess can create skeletal and other problems. Some cats may become quite ill if given too much. They are unable to digest its lactose content. However, small amounts may be appreciated as a treat. Goat's milk, diluted condensed milk and low-lactose milks are better than cow's milk.

kitten can be slowly weaned onto the adult types. There are also special brands available from vets for any kitten or cat that may have a dietary problem as well as special diets for the older cat. These may need lower ratios of certain ingredients, such as proteins and sodium, so as to reduce the workload of the liver.

Flavours should be rotated so interest in meals is maintained. This also encourages familiarity with different tastes. Naturally, Manx will display a greater liking for certain flavours and brands than for others.

FRESH FOODS
To add greater variety and interest, there are many fresh foods that Manx enjoy. Some will be very helpful in cleaning the teeth and exercising the jaw muscles. All have the benefit of providing different textures and smells that help stimulate the palate. Feed these foods two or three times a week as treats or occasionally as complete meals.

Cooked poultry, including the skin, but minus the bones, is usually a favourite, as is quality raw or cooked mincemeat. Cooked beef on the bone gives the cat something to enjoy. Cooked white fish, as well as tinned tuna or sardines, is an example of an ocean delight. Never feed raw fish; this can prove dangerous, even fatal. Although cats rarely

ESTABLISHING DAILY INTAKE
Quoting amounts needed is impossible because of the varying factors mentioned. The best way to establish requirements is on an actual consumption basis. Place a small amount of food on the dish and see how quickly this is eaten. If all is devoured within a few minutes, add a little more. Repeat this until the kitten/cat is satiated and walks away from its dish. Do likewise at the other meals and you will quickly establish daily intake.

enjoy items such as rice, pasta or cooked vegetables, these can nonetheless be finely chopped and mixed with meats or fish. Some Manx may develop a taste for them. Various cheeses and scrambled or boiled eggs will often be appreciated—but never give raw eggs.

If the diet is balanced and varied, the addition of vitamin and mineral supplements is unnecessary and can actually prove dangerous. While certain of these compounds are released from the body if in excess, others are not. They are stored and can adversely affect efficient metabo-

IMPORTANT DON'TS

- Do not let your cat become a fussy eater. Cats are not born fussy but are made that way by their owners. Your cat will not starve if given the correct food, but it may try to convince you otherwise. However, a cat that refuses all foods offered may be ill. Contact your vet.
- Do not give a cat sweet and sticky foods. These provide no benefit and, if eaten, will negatively affect normal appetite for wholesome foods.
- Do not feed vitamin and mineral supplements to either kittens or adults unless under advice from a veterinary surgeon. Excess vitamins and minerals can be as bad for your cat's health as a lack of them. They will create potentially dangerous cellular metabolic imbalances.
- Do not give any questionable foods, such as those that smell or look 'off.' If in doubt, discard them. Always store foods in cool, darkened cupboards. Be sure all foods from the freezer and refrigerator are fully thawed.

Providing your Manx with a balanced diet is most important to the cat's continued good health and weight. Some kittens will develop heartier appetites than others. Feed each cat as an individual.

lism. If a cat shows loss of condition and disinterest in its food, discuss its diet with a vet.

HOW MUCH TO FEED

Food intake is influenced by many factors. These are the cat's age,

HIGH-QUALITY FOOD

The value of a cat food is determined by its protein/carbohydrate compositions. High-quality foods will contain more protein. The cat is a prime predator and needs a high proportion of protein in its diet.

EAT YOUR HAIRBALLS AWAY

Food companies have developed formulas containing a wholesome fibre blend that moves ingested hair through the cat's digestive tract, thus minimising the occurrence of hairballs. Tests show that feeding these formulas moved 80% more hair through the digestive tract, meaning fewer hairballs!

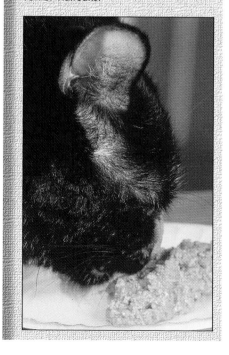

activity level, the ambient temperature (more is eaten in the colder months), the cat's breeding state (rearing kittens) and the quality of the food. Always follow the breeder's recommendations on diet until your kitten has settled into your home. Thereafter the needed quantity will increase as the kitten gets older, until full maturity at about two to three years of age.

As a basic guide, a four-month-old kitten will require four meals a day. At six months old, one meal can be dropped. By twelve months of age, only two meals will be required, possibly only one if dried foods are also available on a free-choice basis. As the number of meals is decreased, the quantity must be increased at the meals fed.

FOOD AND WATER CONTAINERS

Manx are not too fussy over what vessels are used for supplying their food and water, but a few tips are useful. Manx do not like to eat from dirty dishes any more

DIETARY DIFFERENCES BETWEEN CATS AND DOGS

You should never feed your cat dog food because dogs and cats have different dietary needs. Cats have a much higher need for fats than dogs, and kittens need more than adult cats. Cats also require unusually high levels of dietary protein as compared with those required by dogs. The foods you choose for your cat must supply these essential components.

than you would. Their food bowls should be washed after each meal. Water containers should be washed and replenished every day. Saucers make ideal food plates. Wide feeders from your pet shop are excellent for dried biscuits. Pot or polished metal containers are better buys than plastic. They last longer and are easier to keep clean.

The Manx does not like to place its head into deep food dishes nor do they like their whiskers to touch the inner walls. Ensure dishes are wide and shallow.

WHERE AND WHEN TO FEED

Usually, the best place to feed a cat is in the kitchen. It is important to place food and water dishes as far away from the litter tray as possible. This could otherwise deter the cat from eating. Cats also like to eat in quiet comfort. Meals should be spread across the entire day. When the number is reduced to two, these should be given in the morning and evening at convenient times. For the Manx given outdoor freedom, it is best to feed the main meal in the evening. This encourages it to come home at this time. It can then be kept indoors overnight.

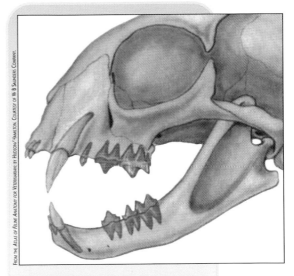

FROM THE *ATLAS OF FELINE ANATOMY FOR VETERINARIANS* BY HUDSON/HAMILTON, COURTESY OF W B SAUNDERS COMPANY.

MEET THE MEAT-EATERS

Since cats are carnivorous, their teeth are designed to bite and cut. Except for crunching dried foods, cats do very little chewing. They have the fewest teeth of any common domestic mammal— typically 30 (although there are some variations). The canines usually are more developed than the incisors.

From the perspective of grooming, the Shorthaired Manx has an easy non-matting coat. If brushed every day it will rarely need combing, though this is beneficial. Brisk brushing followed by a polish, using a chamois leather or piece of silk cloth, will maintain the fur in super condition. If you frequently stroke your Manx, the natural oils on your hand will give the coat a sleek look.

If you have a Longhaired Manx, you will need to pay more attention to the coat. Mats can form that will prevent dead hair from being shed. These will soon enough become entangled with other debris—grass, small sticks, cat litter and even food. If done regularly, grooming will help bond the cat to its owner. The cat will always be a joy to behold and its owner will be very proud.

Regular grooming also enables close examination of the cat for any signs of problems. These include fleas or mites, small wounds, abrasions, swellings and bald areas. The grooming process should include inspection of the cat's ears, teeth and nails.

BRUSHING
Place the cat on a table of a height enabling you to comfortably control and groom the kitty. It can be useful to place white paper on the table. If any fleas are present,

CLEAN CATS
Cats are self-groomers. They use their barbed tongues and front paws for grooming. Some cats never groom themselves, while others spend up to a third of their waking hours grooming themselves. Licking stimulates certain skin glands that make the coat waterproof.

you will more easily notice them if they are groomed out of the fur. If the grooming is carried out gently, cats enjoy the experience. You should start when your Manx is still a kitten. Commence by brushing the fur on the back of the neck. Work along the back and down the sides, then down the legs and finally the tail. The abdominal area must be brushed more gently as it is very sensitive.

Next, repeat the process using the fine-toothed comb, then comb against the lie of the hair. This will enable you to see if there are any parasites present. These often favour the tail base or the neck behind the ears. Next, comb with the lie of the fur. Add a final lustre by brushing with the chamois.

BATHING

Occasionally, even shorthaired cats may need bathing. If yours is a Longhaired Manx, it will need to be bathed more frequently than a Shorthair. Baths may be of the wet or dry type. For wet baths, using the kitchen sink is preferable to a bath. This saves bending and allows for better control of the cat. To prevent the cat from sliding, use a rubber mat. A spray attachment is more efficient than a jug to wet and rinse the coat. The cat should have its own towels.

The choice of shampoo is important. It should ideally be

GROOMING EQUIPMENT

The following will be required for complete grooming:

1. Round-ended, cushioned pin brush
2. Bristle brush
3. Medium-toothed metal comb with handle
4. Flea comb
5. A pair of guillotine nail clippers
6. Powder (If the cat is dark coloured, a soft chamois leather is useful for show grooming.)
7. Supply of cotton wool and cotton buds
8. Plastic pouring jug
9. Spray attachment for taps
10. Cat shampoo (Those for dogs are not suitable for felines. A baby shampoo can be used but is not as effective as one formulated for cats.)
11. One or two quality towels
12. Good hair dryer (the quieter, the better)
13. Non-slip rubber mat
14. Good-sized plastic bowl with a rubber mat placed inside (to use as bath if sink is not suitable)
15. Medium-soft toothbrush and feline toothpaste (A saline solution is an alternative, but is less tasty.)
16. An appropriately sized plastic or other container in which to keep kitty's boutique apparel

formulated for cats—do not use one for dogs. This could cause problems on a cat's coat. Baby shampoos are the best alternative. Dry shampoos in powder form are available from pet shops. Alternatives would be talcum powder, powdered chalk or heated bran flakes.

The kitten should be bathed by the time it is six months of age. This will familiarise it with the process before it matures and the process degenerates into a pitched battle. Cats have no love of bathing but can come to accept it if it does not become an unpleasant ordeal.

Grooming should always precede bathing, as this will remove any dead hairs. With a Longhaired Manx, if any mats should be found in the coat, these must be teased out using the index finger and thumb of both hands. Be very careful not to pull away from the skin while doing this. It will be painful and the cat will object. Never bath a cat that has even the smallest of mats in its fur. Once soaked, these will shrink into tight balls that will be much harder to tease apart.

The key to success lies in ensuring that no water or shampoo is allowed to enter and irritate the eyes or ears. You should be able to cope single-handedly with a kitten. However, it may be prudent to have someone else present just in case the adult proves more of a super cat than a kitten!

Always be gentle when grooming your Manx. Most cats enjoy the experience of brushing, especially if done in a calm and gentle manner.

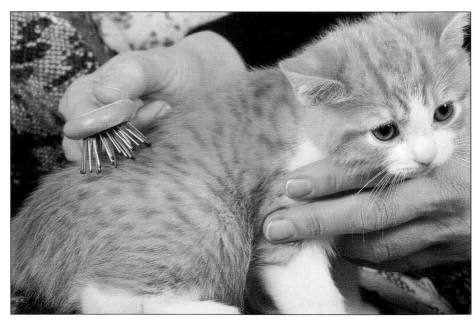

The water temperature should be warm, never cold or too hot. Prepare a shampoo and water solution before commencing. Have a large towel at hand. Commence by soaking the fur of the neck, then work along the back, sides, legs and tail. Pour shampoo onto the back and work this in all directions until the cat has been fully shampooed. Next, thoroughly rinse all the shampoo away. It is essential that none be left otherwise it may cause later irritation. Gently but firmly squeeze all water from the coat. The face can be cleaned using a dampened flannel.

Wrap the kitten in the towel and give it a brisk rubbing until it is as dry as possible. It can then be allowed to dry naturally, after which it can be given a final brush and polish. If the cat is normally allowed outdoors, do

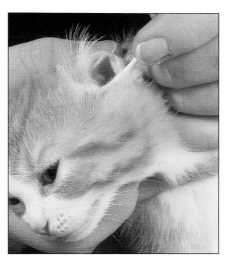

The ears should be cleaned weekly to keep them free of debris. Do not probe with a cotton bud into the ear canal.

not allow this for some hours until you are sure the coat is dry. In the colder months, it is best to attend to bathing in the early evening and keep the cat indoors overnight. The use of a hand dryer is not essential on a short-coated breed, but does shorten the drying time.

DRY SHAMPOO

A dry bath may be preferred to a wet one during very cold weather or when the cat is not well enough for a water bath. Sprinkle dry shampoo into the coat and give it a good brushing. This will remove excess grease and dirt without being as thorough as a wet bath. Be very sure all the powder is brushed from the fur to avoid potential irritation and consequential scratching.

EARS, EYES AND NAILS

When inspecting the ears, look for any signs of dirt. Debris can be gently wiped away using a dampened cotton bud or one with just a little baby or vegetable oil on it. Never attempt to probe into the ear. If the ear is very waxed, this may indicate any of various health problems. A visit to the vet is recommended. The corner of the eyes can be gently wiped with damp cotton wool to remove any dust that occasionally accumulates.

Examine your Manx's ears to search for parasites. Smell the ear and if an odour is detectable, consult your veterinary surgeon.

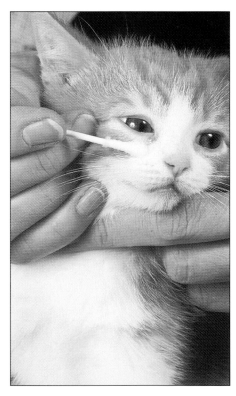

Tear stains can easily be removed with a special solution available from your local pet shop.

Inspection of a cat's claws is achieved by firstly restraining it while on its back on your lap or held against your chest. Hold the paw and apply pressure to the top of this with your thumb. The nail will appear from its sheath. If the nail needs trimming, use the appropriate trimmers.

It is vital you do not cut into,

PRESS-ON NAILS!
A stylish and fairly successful inhibitor of scratching is a plastic covering on the nails. A plastic sheath is placed over each nail and glued on with a strong, permanent adhesive. Depending upon the cat's activity, these sheaths last from one to three months.

or even too close to, the quick, which is a blood vessel. This can be seen as a darker area of the nail in pink-clawed cats. It is more difficult, or not possible, to see the quick in dark-coloured nails. In such instances, trim less. You may need a helper to do the trimming or the holding. If in doubt, let your vet do this for you. If cats have ample access to scratching posts, they will only infrequently, if ever, require their nails to be trimmed.

TEETH

From its youngest days, your kitten should become familiar with having its teeth cleaned. Many owners do not give these the attention they should. This has become progressively more important due to the soft diet

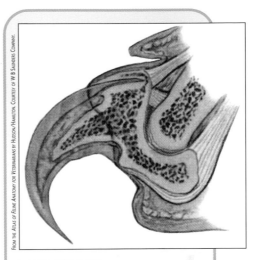

FROM THE *ATLAS OF FELINE ANATOMY FOR VETERINARIANS* BY HUDSON/HAMILTON, COURTESY OF W B SAUNDERS COMPANY.

DECLAWING

Declawing is the surgical removal of all of the claw (or nail) and the first toe joint. This practice is heavily frowned upon and even illegal in some countries, such as the United Kingdom. Unfortunately, in some areas of the world this procedure is still performed. Some owners only have the claws from the front feet removed; others do all four feet. An alternative surgical procedure is removing the tendon that allows the cat to protract its claws. This procedure, referred to as a tendonectomy, as compared to an onychectomy (removal of the claws), is less traumatic for the cat. Claws still must be filed and trimmed after a tendonectomy.

Declawing is not always 100% successful. In two-thirds of the cases, the cats recovered in 72 hours. Only 4–5% of the cats hadn't recovered within a fortnight. About 3% of the cats had their claws grow back!

Keep your Manx's nails short and you will have fewer problems with scratching in your home.

regimens of modern cats. Initially, gently rub the kitten's teeth using a soft cloth on which feline toothpaste has been placed. This will accustom the kitten to having its teeth touched as well as to the taste of the tooth cleaner. When this is no problem for the kitten, you can progress to a soft toothbrush and ultimately one of medium hardness. Periodically let your vet check the cat's mouth.

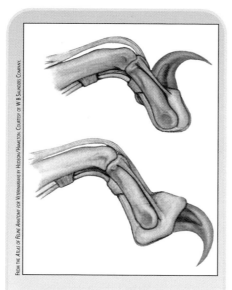

FROM THE ATLAS OF FELINE ANATOMY FOR VETERINARIANS BY HUDSON/HAMILTON. COURTESY OF W B SAUNDERS COMPANY.

RETRACTABLE CLAWS

When at rest, a cat's claws are retracted. The muscles hold the claws in their sheaths. The claw is then extended if the cat wishes to attack prey, defend itself, grab an object or climb. That is why your cat's claws are not always visible. This is true for all species of felines except the cheetah, which is unable to retract its claws, except when it is very young.

GINGIVITIS (Plasmocytic-Lymphocytic Stomatitis)

There are many causes of this condition. But the end result is the same—bad breath, excessive plaque, tooth loss and, almost certainly, pain. The cat salivates excessively, starts to eat less and consequently loses weight. On inspection, the gums are swollen, especially in the area of the premolar and molar teeth. They bleed easily. There are various treatments, such as antibiotics, immunostimulants and disinfectant mouth gels. However, these invariably prove short-term and merely delay the inevitable treatment of extraction.

Prevention avoids this painful condition. Regular tooth inspection and cleaning, plus provision of hard-food items, such as cat biscuits, achieve this to a large extent. There are also special cat chews made of dried fish that help clean the teeth. They also contain antibacterial enzymes that minimise or prevent secondary bacteria from accumulating. Ask for these at your pet shop or vet's surgery. Gingivitis may commence in kittens, so do not think it is something that only occurs in older cats.

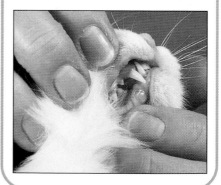

MANX CAT

One of the outstanding virtues of cats is that they are easy to live with. They are fastidious in their personal habits related to grooming and toilet routines and basically require very little of their owners. Nonetheless, behavioural problems in cats can occur, and an owner needs to understand all the possible causes and solutions. You may never encounter a single problem with your cat, but it pays to be prepared should your feline charge disrupt your domestic bliss.

THE BASIS OF TRAINING

The most effective means of training a cat is via reinforcement of success. A cat learning from lavish praise of doing what is required will want to repeat the action to gain more affection. There are no potential negative side effects. Conversely, when scolding or another method of discipline is used, there is always the possibility the cat will not relate the punishment to what the owner had intended.

For example, you cannot discipline for something done in the past. The past is anything much longer than a few minutes ago. If you call the cat to you and

SETTING THE GROUND RULES

From the outset you must determine the ground rules and stick to them. Always remember that your companion's patterns of behaviour begin to form from the moment it first arrives at your home. If the future adult is not to be given outdoor freedom, then do not let it outdoors as a kitten. If any rooms are to be out of bounds to the adult, then do not let the kitten into them. Stability is vital in a cat's life; without it, the result will be stress and its related behavioural changes.

Ground rules of how to handle the kitten and to respect its privacy when sleeping should be instilled into all children. The cat's meals should be given at about the same time each day. This will have the secondary advantage that the pet's toilet habits will be more predictable.

REMEDIAL METHODS

When faced with a problem, firstly try to pinpoint the likely cause(s). Next, consider the remedial options. Be sure these will not result in negative side effects linked to you. Always be the paragon of patience. Some problems may be extremely complex and deeply rooted within the cat's behaviour patterns. As such, they are habits not easily changed, and often difficult to analyse. In discussing the following problems, it is hoped that you will understand the basic ways to correct other unwanted patterns of behaviour that might occur. But always remember that it is far better to avoid a problem than to correct it.

WHY WHISKERS?

Cats are famous for their whiskers. The whiskers are tactile hairs by which cats feel. Most tactile hairs are on the cat's face, mostly on the upper lip and around the eyes, and on the wrist (carpus). These carpal hairs are extremely sensitive and are found on many predatory animals that use their front paws for holding their victims.

THE TRUTH ABOUT CATS AND DOGS

Cats are unique in having the scrotum fully haired, a marked difference from their canine counterparts. This led one early observer to say that cats were not small dogs! Dogs were domesticated well before cats since cats only served to protect the abode of the owner from rodents, while dogs served as guards, hunters, herders, exterminators and as loyal companions that were readily trainable. Cats have always been more independent and less trainable.

reprimand it for something done hours earlier, it cannot relate to that action. It will relate the discipline to the act of going to you when called! This will create insecurity in the pet, increasing the risk that more problems will develop.

THE LITTER TRAY

A very common problem for some owners is that their cat starts to attend to its toileting needs anywhere other than in its litter tray. The problem may become apparent from the time the kitten gets to its new home, or it may develop at any time during its life. So, let us start from the beginning and try and avoid the situation.

Until you are satisfied the kitten is using its litter tray, do not give it access to carpeted rooms. The youngster should already have been litter trained well before you obtained it. You should buy a litter tray similar to the one it is already familiar with. It is also important that the same brand of litter is used, at least initially. Place the tray in a quiet spot so the kitten has privacy when attending its needs.

A kitten will need to relieve itself shortly after it has eaten, exercised or slept. Watch it carefully at these times. If it stoops to attend to its needs other than in the litter tray, calmly lift it into its tray and scratch at the litter. Never shout or panic the kitty by making a sudden rush for it. If it does what is hoped, give it lots of praise. If it steps out of the tray, gently place it back in for a few seconds.

If nothing happens, be patient and wait, then repeat the process. If it fouls the kitchen floor when you are not watching, simply

CAUSES OF LITTER-BOX PROBLEMS

1. The litter tray is dirty. Cats never like to use a previously fouled tray.
2. The litter has been changed to one of a different texture that the cat does not like. Generally the finer-grained litters are the most favoured.
3. A scented litter is being used to mask odours. The cat may not like the scent. Such litters should not be necessary if the tray is regularly cleaned.
4. The tray is regularly cleaned, but an ammonium or pine-based disinfectant is being used. This may aggravate the cat's sensitive nasal mucous membranes. Additionally, the phenols in pine are dangerous to cats.
5. The litter tray is located too close to the cat's food and water bowls. Cats do not like to eat near litter trays or to defecate/urinate close to their feeding areas.
6. Another cat or free-roaming pet has been added to the household and is causing the cat stress. In multi-cat households, two or more trays may be needed.
7. There is insufficient litter in the tray. There should be about 2 inches of litter depth.
8. The cat has developed a fear of using the tray due to an upsetting experience. For instance, the owner may have caught the cat as it finished using the tray in order that it could be given a medicine. Children may be disturbing it while it is relieving itself.
9. The cat is ill (or elderly) and is unable to control its bowel movements. Veterinary attention is required.
10. The cat, because of one or more of the previous problems, has established other more favourable areas.

TIDY TOILETING

During the kitten's stay in the nest box, the mother will assist or even stimulate bowel and urine elimination, at least for the first month of the kitten's life. The mother also does the clean-up work in the nest box. But once the kitten is older, it becomes capable of relieving itself out of the nest box. Usually the kitten likes sand, soft earth or something that seems absorbent and is easily moved with its paws. By the time the kitten is two months old, it should develop the discipline of covering its elimination. Not all kittens develop this discipline, though the use of an absorbent clay litter seems to be helpful in developing this discipline in young cats. Your local pet shop will have various cat litters to offer you.

this is only part of the solution. Next, the habit of fouling other places must be overcome. Where possible, do not let the cat enter rooms it has started to foul until the odour has had time to fully disperse. Wash the area of the accident, then treat carpets and soft furnishings with an odour neutraliser (not an air freshener) from your pet shop or vet.

If the cat cannot be prevented from entering certain rooms, then cover previously fouled areas with plastic sheeting or tinfoil, or rinse the fouled area with white vinegar (which cats hate!). Also, place a litter tray in the fouled room while the retraining is underway.

clean this up and wait for the next opportunity to transport the kitten to its tray. It rarely takes long for a kitten to consistently use this. Be very sure the tray is kept spotless. Cats have no more desire to use a fouled toilet than you do. Every few days give the cat tray a good wash using soapy water and always rinse it thoroughly. Allow it to dry, then fill the tray with litter to depth of about 4–6 cms (1.5–2 inches).

By identifying the cause(s) of litter-box problems, the correction is often self-evident. However, once the cause has been corrected,

MARKING TERRITORY

Cats are geographical by nature and they mark their territories in the usual way...by spraying their urine. The frequency of spraying is amazing! A non-breeding male cat that is not within its own turf will spray about 13 times an hour while travelling through the new territory. A breeding male will spray almost twice as much. One reports states that free-ranging males spray 62.6 times an hour—that's more than once a minute!

Cat urine is recognisable for at least 24 hours and male cats spend a lot of time sniffing the area. Females spend less time, but both sexes easily recognise the urine from male cats that are strange to the area.

It may help if a different size, type or shape of tray is used.

SCENT MARKING

Both sexes scent mark, though males are more prolific. It is a means of advertising their presence in a territory, thus an integral part of their natural behaviour. Spraying is usually done against a vertical surface. It tells other males that the individual is residing in that territory. Alternatively, it will tell a female that a male lives close

Indoor cats may mark the furniture if not properly trained. Such bad habits much to be curtailed immediately. Breeding animals and outdoor cats are more inclined to mark than are everyday indoor cats.

by—or, with the female, it will tell the male that a female is in the area. It is thus a very important part of every cat's social language.

Neutered cats have little need to mark their territory or leave their 'calling card' to attract mates. They are far less likely to spray than those not altered. However, scent marking may commence when the cat is attempting to assert its position in the household.

To overcome the problem of scent marking, you first need to try and identify if there is an obvious specific cause. In multi-cat households, it also requires positive identification of the sprayer(s) and the favoured spraying surface. Giving the cat more freedom may help, and its own sleeping place if it does not have one. Covering the sprayed surface with plastic sheeting, or a cloth impregnated with a scent the cat does not like (such as lemon, pepper or bleach) may be

FERAL CATS

Feral cats are, as a general rule, undernourished. They spend most of their time searching for food. Consequently, those feral cats that have kittens spend less time with their kittens than do well-nourished cats. It has been shown that kittens born to feral mothers are usually unsocial and show little affection for their mothers. Obviously, they would show a similar lack of affection for a human. That's one of the reasons that feral kittens make poor pets and should neither be adopted nor brought into your home. Kittens, which for any reason are separated from their mothers at the age of two weeks, develop an attitude of fear and wariness. They escape from contact with other cats or humans and can even be dangerous if they feel trapped.

CAUSES OF SCENT MARKING

1. Another cat, or pet, has been introduced to the household. It may be bullying the resident cat. This problem may resolve itself when the two get to know each other. The more cats there are, the longer it may take for the situation to be resolved. Much will depend on the space within which the cats may roam and whether they are able to avoid those they dislike.
2. The birth of a new family member may annoy the cat for a while, especially if its owner suddenly gives it less attention.
3. A friend staying in the home for a few days may not like cats. If 'shooed' away a number of times, the cat may feel it should assert its position and mark it.
4. If the cat is given outdoor freedom, a bully may have moved into the territory. Having lost control of its own garden, the pet may assert its territorial boundaries within its home. If a cat flap is used, another cat may be entering the home and this will trigger the resident to scent mark.

successful. Spraying the cat with a water pistol when catching it in the action is a common ploy. Veterinary treatment with the hormone progesterone may prove effective—discuss this with your vet.

SCRATCHING
Scratching is a normal feline characteristic. Unfortunately, house cats tend to destroy the furniture to satisfy their need to

A lovely brown tabby and white Manx kitten with nicely defined markings. This is a popular colour variety.

MAN MEETS CAT

Early man, perhaps 8000 years ago, started his symbiotic relationship with domestic cats, *Felis catus* or *Felis domesticus.* The cats killed and ate the rats and mice and probably anything else which crawled and was small, which early man attracted and considered as pests. Early man reciprocated by allowing the cat to sleep in his cave, hut or tent. Cats, being essentially nocturnal, kept the small mammals (rats, mice, etc.) from disturbing the sleep of early man.

As early man evolved to modern man, the domestic cat came along as an aid to pest control. This was especially true of peoples who farmed, as farmers were plagued with rodents. Though most cats were not selectively bred for their predatory skills, it was obvious that those cats that were the best hunters were more successful in evolutionary terms than the cats that were more meek. Modern cats have changed very little from the cats from which they descended. There are still, today, cats that are very predatory, attacking small mammals and birds; there are also meek cats which, unless fed by their owners, would perish in a competitive cat society.

It has been shown repeatedly that if kittens are socialised in a proper manner, they will become peaceful pets. This includes lions and tigers. If the kittens are not socialised properly, they revert immediately to their aggressive, predatory behaviours.

scratch. Feral or outdoor cats usually attack a tree because trees are readily accessible and the bark of the tree suits their needs perfectly. If the outdoor cat lives in a pride, it will scratch more than a solitary feral cat. The reasons for this are known. When cats scratch, they leave telltale marks. Parts of the nail's sheath exudate from glands located between their claws, and the visual aspects are the marks

CATS AND OTHER PETS

If you already have a pet cat or cats, or dogs, or almost any other animal that isn't small, creeping or crawling, your cat can usually be socialised so the other pet and the cat will tolerate each other. In many cases, cats and dogs become quite friendly and attached to each other, often making frequent physical contacts, sleeping together or even sharing each other's food.

which cats leave to impress or advertise their presence.

Cat owners whose cats scratch should not consider the scratching as an aggressive behavioural disorder. It is normal for cats to scratch. Keeping your cat's claws clipped or filed so they are as short as possible without causing bleeding may inhibit scratching. Your vet can teach you how to do this. Clipping and filing should be started when the kitten is very young. Starting this when the cat has matured is much more difficult and may even be dangerous.

There are ways to control annoying cat scratching. Certainly, the easiest way is to present your cat with an acceptable scratching post. These are usually available at most pet shops. The post should be covered with a material that is to your cat's liking. If your cat has already indicated what it likes to scratch, it usually is a good idea to cover the post with this same material. Veterinary surgeons often suggest that you use sandpaper, as this will reduce the cat's nails quickly and it will not have the urge to scratch. Certainly using hemp, carpeting, cotton towelling or bark is worth a try. Once the cat uses the post, it usually will have neither a desire nor a need to scratch anyplace else.

Besides the physical need to scratch, many cats have a psychological need to scratch. This is evidenced by where they scratch versus what they scratch. Often cats prefer semi-darkness. Some prefer flat surfaces and not vertical surfaces. Some prefer public areas in which their

SCRATCHING FURNITURE

All cats need to scratch in order to maintain their claws in good condition. For this reason, one or more scratching posts strategically placed in the cat's most-used rooms will normally prevent the problem. Place the post in front of the scratched furniture. It can be moved steadily further away once the furniture is ignored. This is a problem that may become more manifest when cats that are not allowed outdoors have insufficient indoor provisions to scratch.

human friends are present instead of secluded areas. It may be stress-related, as with scent marking, because scratching is another territorial marking behaviour. In any case, the idea is to get your cat to scratch the post and not the carpets, furniture, drapes or the duvet on your bed.

Introduce your cat to the post by rubbing its paws on the post, hoping it will take the hint. Oftentimes the cat voluntarily attacks the post. Unfortunately, oftentimes it doesn't. If you catch

Provide your kitten with safe toys that you can purchase from your pet shop. Do not offer your kitten homemade toys, as these can be dangerous.

your cat scratching in a forbidden area, startle it with a loud shout, banging a folded newspaper against your hand or doing something that will take its attention away from scratching. *Never* hit the cat. This will only get a defensive reaction that might be counterproductive.

RUBBISH RUMMAGING

Cats are inquisitive and may decide to have a good look through any interesting rubbish bins that are exuding an enticing odour. Normally, the answer is to remove the bin. However, if the attraction always seems to be kitchen rubbish, there may be a nutritional problem. The cat may be searching for food because it is being underfed! It may alternatively be receiving an unbalanced diet and is trying to satisfy its inner need for a given missing ingredient.

Another possibility, and one that may be more appropriate to the indoors-only cat, is boredom or loneliness. These conditions can only be remedied by greater interaction between owner and cat

THE PICA SYNDROME

The term 'pica' is a veterinary term that refers to a morbid desire to ingest things that are abnormal to the cat's diet. Cats are often addicted to soft materials like wool, silk, cotton or a mixture of these and synthetic cloths. Hard plastics, wood and even metals have been involved in this pica syndrome. If you observe your cat chewing these fabrics or materials, speak to your vet. Most vets who observe the pica syndrome think it is a nervous problem that can successfully be treated with drugs normally used for depression. In any case, the genetic makeup of your cat should be investigated and if pica occurs in any of the parents or previous offspring, do not breed your cat.

CAT SCRATCH DISEASE

An objectionable habit of many poorly raised kittens is their exuberant jumping to greet you. This flying jump may result in the kitten's being attached to your body; otherwise it will fall to the floor and may injure itself. In the attachment process, your skin will usually be pierced, and this is a health concern. All cat scratches and bites should be thoroughly cleaned with an antiseptic soap. If a sore appears at the site of the wound, you should visit your family doctor immediately.

Cat scratch disease is a well-known problem. It is caused by a bacterium (*Rochalimaea henselae*) that is usually easily treated with antibiotics. However, more and more cases show resistance to the usual antibiotics.

Untreated cat scratch fever may result in an enlargement of the lymph nodes, imitating a cancerous condition known as lymphoma. Interestingly enough, the lymph nodes, upon biopsy, may show large Reid-Sternberg cells, which are a characteristic of Hodgkins lymphoma. The bottom line is that cat scratches should be taken seriously.

The Manx is very expressive with its claws! Training your Manx where and when to use its claws is the best remedy for its scratching furniture or draperies.

and/or obtaining a companion feline.

Clearly the cause should be identified. The immediate solution is to place the rubbish in a cupboard or similar place that is out of the cat's reach. This type of solution is called removal of the re-enforcer. It is a common method of overcoming problems across a number of unwanted behaviours. However, it does not correct the underlying problem that must still be addressed.

The first-time cat owner should not think that all of the problems discussed will likely be encountered. They are only met when the cat's environment is lacking in some way. Always remember that the older cat may have problems with bowel control. An extra litter tray at another location in the home will usually remedy this situation. Finally, if a problem is found and you are not able to remedy it, do seek the advice of your vet or breeder.

Breeding Your

MANX CAT

While the idea of becoming a breeder may appeal to many owners, the reality is more difficult than is often appreciated. It requires dedication, considerable investment of time and money, and the ability to cope with many heart-wrenching decisions and failures.

It would be quite impossible to discuss the complexities of practical breeding in only one chapter, so we will consider the important requirements of being a breeder plus some basic feline reproductive information. This will enable you to better determine if, indeed, this aspect of the hobby is for you.

BEING A BREEDER

Apart from great affection for the breed, a successful breeding programme requires quantifiable objectives. Foremost among these is the rearing of healthy kittens free from known diseases. Next is the desire to produce offspring that are as good as, indeed better than, their parents.

Such objectives ensure that a breeder will endeavour to maintain standards and reduce or remove from the breed population any instances of dangerous diseases

TOO MANY CATS

There are already too many cats in the world. In many countries, thousands of pathetic-looking felines can be seen wandering the streets in a badly emaciated state. They live tormented lives and have become a major social problem in many areas. There can be no excuse for these feral populations in developed Western nations. Quite frankly, some people who own cats, including some pedigreed owners, lack a sense of responsibility.

Cats allowed to roam in a non-neutered state are by far the main reason for the overpopulation problem. Unless a cat is of show or breeding quality, there is not a single justification for it to be bred or to remain in a non-neutered state. If your cat was purchased as a pet, you should help to resolve this global problem by having it neutered at the earliest possible date. This will make it a far healthier, happier and less problematic pet.

and conditions. Only stock registered and tested free of major diseases should ever be used. Adopting such a policy helps to counteract those who breed from inferior and often unhealthy cats.

To be a successful breeder you will need to become involved in the show competition side of the

disadvantages should also be carefully considered. Kittens are demanding, especially once they are over three weeks of age. Rearing, vaccination, registration and veterinary bills will be costly. Any thoughts of profit should be dispelled. Homes must be found for the kittens, which will entail receiving many telephone calls—some at very inconvenient hours.

Many potential buyers will prove to be either unsuitable or 'time wasters' looking for the cheapest pedigreed cat obtainable. Kittens may die, while cats of any age could test positive for a major disease. They may have to be put to sleep or given to a caring person who understands the problem.

Owning a number of cats will mean investing in cat pens. When females come into heat, they will try to escape and mate with any local tom with a twinkle in his eye! Their scent

hobby. Only via this route will you be able to determine if your programme is successful or not. Always remember that even the top-winning breeders still produce quite a high percentage of kittens that will only be of pet quality. There will be many disappointments along the road to even modest success.

THE DISADVANTAGES OF BREEDING

There are many rewards to be gained from breeding but the

and calls will attract roving Romeos who will gather near your home and involve themselves in a series of raucous battles. Holidays and matings will need to be planned around hoped-for litter dates. All in all, owning even one or two breeding females is a major commitment.

Before deciding whether breeding really is something you want to undertake, what would make good sense would be to neuter the pet and then become an exhibitor. When you have exhibited a number of times, your knowledge of cats will be greater, as will your contacts. You will be more aware of what quality is all about, and what it will cost for a well-bred female. It will be like an apprenticeship. Whether you then become a breeder, remain an exhibitor or prefer life as a pet owner, you will be glad you heeded the words of advice given here.

STOCK SELECTION

Stock selection revolves around health, quality, sex and age. Before these are discussed, it should be stated that many beginners unwisely rush this process. It is essential that ample time be devoted to researching from whom to purchase. This decision will influence all of a novice breeder's future endeavours.

TOM FOOLERY

A non-neutered male cat kept as a single pet has little or no value for breeding purposes. It must be exhibited so it can gain some fame. The owner must have modern facilities to house both males and females. Females are always serviced at the home of the stud owner. This is extra responsibility and cost.

Such a male cannot be given any freedom to roam. If the tom is kept indoors, its scent-marking odours will often become intolerable. Even kept outdoors in a suitable cat pen, it will spray regularly to attract the attention of any females in the area. Toms are more assertive and often more aggressive than neutered males.

If they are allowed any outdoor freedom, they will become involved in battles with the local toms. Consequently, they will soon lose their handsome looks! Most cat breeders do not even keep males because of the problems and costs they entail. These cats are best kept in catteries where the owners have the time, the funds and everything else needed to justify their retention.

THE MALE STUD

The selection of a suitable stud should have been planned months before, as it can take some time to find the best male to use. It is preferred that the breeding lines of the stud are compatible with those of the female, meaning both pedigrees will carry a number of the same individuals in them. This is termed line-breeding. The ideal male will excel in those features that are considered weak in the female. You may read in other books that if a female is weak in a given feature, the ideal stud will be the total opposite. However, this can be misleading.

If the female is weak in a feature, what you do not need is a stud that is excessive in that feature. Rather, his feature should be as near the ideal as possible. Genetically, this will improve that feature in your line without introducing unwanted genetic variance in your stock. Compensatory matings will create such a variance. Once a male has been selected, ensure all his papers and vaccinations are in order. The female will be taken to the stud and left with him for a few days.

HEALTH

Cats should only be obtained from a breeder whose stock has been tested negative for FeLV, FIP and FIV. The stock should be current on all vaccinations and worm treatments. Additionally, its blood type should be known so as to avoid incompatibility problems.

QUALITY

This must come in two forms. One is in the individual cat's appearance; the other is in its genetic ability to pass on the quality of its parents. The best way of obtaining these paired needs is to obtain initial stock from a breeder having a proven record of success with Manx, and with the colour or pattern you plan to start with. Being well acquainted with the breed's standard will be critical when seeking foundation stock. A female show cat attains her titles based on her appearance, but she may not pass on those looks to her offspring. Another cat that is very sound may pass on most of her good points and thus be more valuable for breeding. Of course, all litters will be influenced by the quality of the tom used. He will account for 50% of the offsprings' genes. When viewing a litter of kittens, never forget that they are the result of the genes of two cats.

SEX

The beginner should only obtain females. The best advice is to commence with just one very sound female. By the time you have exhibited her and gained more knowledge about the finer points of the breed, you will be better able to judge what true quality is all about. By then, you will also have made many contacts on the show circuit. Alternatively, you may decide breeding is not for you and will have invested only a minimum of time and money. A male is not needed until a breeder has become established. Even then, owning one is not essential to success. There is no shortage of quality studs available for leasing. Males create many problems that the novice can do without. Once you gain experience, you can decide if owning a male would be of any particular benefit.

AGE
There is no specific age at which stock should be purchased but the following are suggested:
1. Most people purchase young kittens so that they can enjoy them. However, with such youngsters, their ultimate quality is harder to assess.
2. Chances are improved if a kitten has already won awards in shows. This will be when she is 14 weeks to 9 months of age, but she will be more costly.
3. A quality young female that has already produced offspring is a prudent choice, but will be the most expensive option.

THE BREEDING QUEEN
A female used for breeding purposes is called a queen. The principal requirement of such a cat is that she is an excellent example of the breed. This does not mean she must be a show winner. Many a winning exhibition cat has proved to have little breeding value. This is because a show cat gains success purely on its appearance; however, it may not pass those looks to its offspring.

A good breeding female may lack that extra something needed to be a top winner. Yet, she may pass on most of her excellent features to her offspring. Much will depend on the breeding line from which she was produced. Therefore, any potential breeder must research existing breeders to ascertain which have good track records of producing consistently high-quality cats. In truth, and sadly, few newcomers in their haste to become breeders make this extra effort. This can result in becoming disillusioned if the female produces only average to inferior kittens.

THE BREEDING PROCESS

Sexual maturity in cats may come as early as four months of age. Breeding should not be considered until the female is at least 12 months old, especially in the slow-maturing breeds such as those of Persian and European stock ancestry. A young cat barely out of her kitten stage may not have the required physical or psychological stability to produce and raise a vigorous litter. After her first heat, a female will normally come into heat again every two to three weeks and continue to do so until mated. The actual oestrous period lasts three to eight days. It is during this time that she is receptive to a male.

Once the mating has been successful, the time between fertilisation and birth of the young, known as the gestation period, is in the range of 59 to 67 days, 63 or 64 days being typical. The litter size will generally be two to five. Kittens are born blind and helpless, but develop rapidly. Their eyes open about the seventh day. By 21 days, they start exploring. At this time they will also be sampling solid foods. By eight weeks, they can be vaccinated and neutered if required. Weaning normally commences by the age of six weeks and is completed within two to three weeks. Manx kittens can go to their new homes after four months af age. During this period you must decide if you wish to register the kittens or merely 'declare' them. This allows them to be registered at a later time. Obtain the necessary information and forms from your cat-registration authority. You should also consider the benefits of registering your own breeder prefix. This, however, is only worthwhile if you intend to breed on a more than casual basis. If you have decided that certain kittens are unsuitable for showing/ breeding, do consider early neutering.

Exhibiting Your
MANX CAT

Without shows, the cat fancy could not exist. There would be only a handful of breeds as compared with today's ever-growing list. There would be fewer colour patterns and far less public awareness of cat-related issues. Given the great importance of shows to the cat fancy, it is perhaps a little surprising, and disappointing, that the majority of cat owners have never even visited a feline exhibition.

Shows such as the National and the Supreme of Britain, or their equivalents in other countries, are the shop windows of the world of domestic cats. They are meeting places where breeders from all over the country compete to determine how well their breeding programmes are developing. A show is also a major social event on the cat calendar.

Whether a potential pet owner or breeder of the future, you should visit one or two shows. It can be a great day out for the whole family. Apart from the wonderful selection of breeds, there are also many trade stands. If a product is available, it will be seen at the large exhibitions. Many of the national clubs and magazines have stands.

The two major shows mentioned are held in the winter months, usually November and

BECOMING AN EXHIBITOR

Before any hobbyist enters a show, he is advised to join a local cat club. Here, hobbyists will meet local breeders who will not only assess their cats for them but also provide help on many other topics. The novice exhibitor could attend one or two shows with an exhibitor in order to learn the ropes. During this period, he can become familiar with the show rules and regulations. These are quite extensive, intended to safeguard the best interests of the hobby, the exhibitors and, most importantly, the cats.

It is of interest to note that some breeders own cats in partnership with other fanciers. This is useful when one person enjoys the breeding side and the other the exhibition side. It enables both to really be involved in the hobby to a level that might not have been possible for either on his own. So, whether you fancy being an exhibitor or you just love cats, do make a point of visiting the next show in your area.

December. However, there are hundreds of other shows staged during the year in various parts of the country. They range from small local club events to major championship breed shows and are usually advertised in the cat magazines. Your ruling cat association can also supply a list of shows.

SHOW ORGANISATION

So that you will have some idea of how things are organised, the following information will be helpful. You will learn even more by purchasing the show catalogue. This contains the names and addresses of the exhibitors and details of their cats. It also lists the prizes, indicates the show regulations and carries many interesting advertisements.

A major show revolves around three broad categories of cats:

1. Unaltered cats, meaning those that are capable of breeding.
2. Neuters.
3. Non-pedigreed cats.

There is, thus, the opportunity for every type of cat, from the best of Manx to the everyday 'moggie' pets, to take part. These three broad categories are divided into various sections. For example, the unaltered and neuters are divided into their respective sections, such as Longhair, Semi-Longhair, British, Foreign, Siamese and so on.

There are many more classes other than those mentioned. These include club classes and those for kittens and non-pedigreed cats.

EXAMPLES OF CLASSES AT SHOWS

Open	Any cat of the specified breed.
Novice	Cats that have never won a first prize.
Limit	Cats that have not won more than first prizes.
Junior	Cats over nine months of age but less than two years on the day of the show.
Senior	Cats over two years old.
Visitors	Cats living a given distance away from the show venue.
Assessment	Experimental breeds, which have an approved standard.
Aristocrat	Cats with one or two Challenge Certificates (or Premiers for neuters) so are not yet full Champions/Premiers.

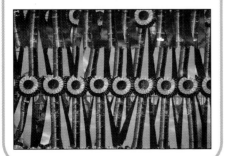

JUDGING

There are two ways cats can be judged. One is pen judging, the other is bench or ring judging. In Britain, pen judging is the normal method, though bench judging is used for Best in Show. In pen judging, the judge moves around the cat pens. The cat gaining the most points when compared to the standard wins. In bench judging, stewards take the cats to the judge.

If a cat wins its class, it then competes against other class winners. By this process of elimination, a cat may go on to win the Best of Breed award. It then competes against other breed winners for the Best in Group award. The group winners compete for the Best in Show award.

A breeder can gather a number of awards during the course of a show. Even those who do not own the very best cats can take pride in gaining second, third, fourth and recommended, especially if won at the larger shows. By progression, the top cat at a show will win its class, its breed, its section, and ultimately will become the Best in Show

CLASSES FOR NON-PEDIGREED CATS

For non-pedigreed cats there are many classes, which include those for single colours, bicolours, tabbies, half-pedigreed, and so on. In this section are many delightful classes, such as those for cats owned by senior citizens, by young children (by age group), best original stray or rescued cat, best personality, most unusual looking, most photogenic and best older cat. Within this cat section can be seen some truly gorgeous felines. There is no doubt that the pet classes have been the springboard that has launched many a top breeder into the world of pedigreed cats.

'VETTING IN'

In England, cats are examined by a veterinary surgeon upon arrival to a show to make sure that they appear healthy. This process is called 'vetting in.' If the cat is rejected, it can not be exhibited again until it receives a 'clearance certificate.' The reasons for rejection are stated in the rule book, which can be obtained at the show.

exhibit. The titles a cat can win commence with that of Champion, or Premier in the case of neuters. A Grand Champion is made after winning in competition with others of its same status. The same applies to a Grand Premier. The judging system may vary from one country to another but the basis remains as outlined.

THE SHOW CAT

When a cat is seen preening in its pen, the hard work that has gone into its preparation is rarely appreciated. Exhibits must be in peak condition and their coats in full bloom. The potential exhibit must be gradually trained to spend hours within its show pen. It must display no fear or aggression towards strangers, such as the stewards or the judges. These must be able to physically examine it, including its ears and teeth; it also involves being lifted into the air. If a cat scratches or bites a judge, or any other show official, it is automatically withdrawn from the show. A repeat of this in the future would result, in most instances, in the cat's show career being terminated by the ruling association.

Apart from being comfortable with people peering into its pen, the cat must be able to endure long journeys to the show venue. Unless trained, the cat may become a nervous, aggressive feline that will have a very short show career.

Obviously, the cat must display quality. This means having none of the major faults that would prevent it from gaining a first prize. These are listed in the breed standard. The meaning of quality is very subjective. You do not need to own a potential champion to be a successful exhibitor. The cat must also be registered with the association under whose rules the show is being run. In Britain this will be the Governing Council of the Cat Fancy (GCCF) or The Cat Association of Britain.

As in all competitive events, exhibits can gain prizes at the lower levels of a hobby without having any realistic chance of awards in the major shows. Owning such exhibits is often part of a top breeder/exhibitor's portfolio from his early days in the hobby. Others may never move beyond the smaller shows but still gain reputations for owning sound stock. They thoroughly enjoy being involved at their given level.

If the idea of exhibiting appeals to you, the best way to make a start is to join a local club. There you not only will be advised on all procedures but also will be able to make many new friends who also love cats. Exhibiting can be costly in cash and time, but you can focus on the more local shows while attending the larger ones as a visitor.

MANX CAT

Maintaining a cat in the peak of good health revolves around the implementation of a sound husbandry strategy. At the basic level, this means being responsible about feeding, cleanliness and grooming. However, in spite of an owner's best efforts in these matters, cats may still become ill due to other causes. Although owners can attempt to prevent, identify and react to problems, only a vet is qualified to diagnose and suggest and/or effect remedies. Attempts by owners or 'informed' friends to diagnose and treat for specific diseases are dangerous and potentially life-threatening to the cat.

SELECTING A VETERINARY SURGEON

Your selection of a veterinary surgeon should not be based upon personality (as most are) but upon convenience to your home. You want a vet who is close because you might have emergencies or need to make multiple visits for treatments. You want a vet who has services that you might require such as nail clipping and bathing, as well as sophisticated pet supplies and a good reputation for ability and responsiveness.

There is nothing more frustrating than having to wait a day or more to get a response from your veterinary surgeon.

All veterinary surgeons are licensed and their diplomas and/or certificates should be displayed in their waiting rooms. There are, however, many veteri-

A LONG, HEALTHY LIFE

As veterinary surgeons make medical advances in the health care of cats, the longevity of the typical house cat is improving. Certainly ages between 15 and 18 years are not uncommon, and reports of cats living more than 20 years are predictable.

nary specialities that usually
require further studies and intern-
ships. There are specialists in
heart problems (veterinary cardiol-
ogists), skin problems (veterinary
dermatologists), teeth and gum
problems (veterinary dentists), eye
problems (veterinary ophthalmol-
ogists) and x-rays (veterinary
radiologists), as well as vets who
have specialities in reproduction,
nutrition and behaviour. Most
veterinary surgeons do routine
surgery, such as neutering and
stitching up wounds. When the
problem affecting your cat is
serious, it is not unusual or
impudent to get another medical
opinion, although in Britain you
are obliged to advise the vets
concerned about this. You might
also want to compare costs among
several veterinary surgeons.
Sophisticated health care and
veterinary services can be very
costly. It is not infrequent that
important decisions are based
upon financial considerations.

PREVENTATIVE MEDICINE
It is much easier, less costly and
more effective to practise preventative medicine than to fight bouts
of illness and disease. Properly
bred kittens come from parents
who were selected based upon
their genetic disease profile. Their
mothers should have been
vaccinated, free of all internal and
external parasites and properly
nourished. For these reasons, a

A tortie and white Manx models as the portrait of good health.

KEEPING YOUR CAT HEALTHY

Although there are a multitude of ailments, diseases and accidents that could befall a cat, all but the most minor of problems can be avoided with good management. The following tips are a recipe for keeping your cat in the peak of health.

- Make sure it is vaccinated and in other ways protected from each of the major diseases. It must also receive annual boosters to maintain immunity.
- Have periodic checks made by your vet to see if your cat has worms.
- Ensure the cat receives an adequate diet that is both appealing and balanced.
- Have the kitten neutered if it is not to be used for breeding.
- Ensure the cat's litter tray, food/water vessels and grooming tools are always maintained in spotless condition.
- Do not let your cat out overnight or when you are away working or shopping.
- Always wash your hands after gardening or petting other people's pets.
- Groom your cat daily. If this is done, you will more readily notice fleas or other problems than if grooming was done less frequently.
- Never try to diagnose and treat problems that are clearly of an internal type. Remember, even the most informed of breeders is not a vet and unable to reliably diagnose problems for you or advise treatments. Contact your vet.
- If you are ever in doubt about the health of your cat, do not delay in discussing your concerns with your vet. Delays merely allow problems to become more established.

visit to the veterinary surgeon who cared for the queen is recommended. The queen can pass on disease resistance to her kittens, which can last for eight to ten weeks. She can also pass on parasites and many infections. That's why you should visit the veterinary surgeon who cared for the queen.

VACCINATIONS

Most vaccinations are given by injection and should only be done by a veterinary surgeon. Both he and you should keep a record of the date of the injection, the identification of the vaccine and the amount given. The first vaccination is normally given when the kitten is about 8–9 weeks old. About 30 days later, a booster is given. Although there are many diseases to which a cat may fall victim, the most dangerous three—FIE, FVR and FeLV—can be safeguarded against with a single (three-in-one) injection. Thereafter an annual booster is all that is required.

MAJOR DISEASES

There are a number of diseases for which there is either no cure or

BLOOD GROUP INCOMPATIBILITY (BGI)

In recent years, blood group incompatibility has become the focus of scientists, vets and breeders. Its importance to pet owners is when transfusions are needed. For breeders, it probably accounts for a large percentage of kittens that die from fading kitten syndrome. Scientifically the problem is called neonatal erythrolysis, meaning the destruction of red blood cells in newly born offspring.

Cats have two blood groups, A & B. Group A is dominant to B (which is genetically called recessive). When the antibodies of B-group mothers are passed to A-group kittens, via her colostrum milk, they destroy red blood cells. Death normally follows within a few days.

Most domestic cats tested are group A. However, national and regional differences display a variation in which 1-6% may be of type B. In pedigreed breeds it has been found that the number of group-B cats varies significantly. The following breeds, based on present available data, have the indicated percentage incidence of group-B blood type.

0%	Siamese, Burmese and Oriental Shorthair
1-5%	Manx, Maine Coon and Norwegian Forest
10-20%	Abyssinian, Birman, Japanese Bobtail, Persian, Scottish Fold and Somali
25-50%	British Shorthair, Devon and Cornish Rex and Exotic Shorthair

The clear implication to breeders is to establish their cats' blood group, via testing, and conduct appropriate matings. These should not result in B-group mothers' nursing A-group kittens.

The safe matings are:

1. Group-A males   x   A females
2. Group-B males   x   A or B females
3. Group-A females x   A or B males
4. Group-B females x   B males

Breeders are advised to seek further information before embarking on stock purchase and breeding programmes.

little chance of recovery. However, some can be prevented by vaccination. All breeders and owners should ensure kittens are so protected.

FELINE INFECTIOUS ENTERITIS (FIE)

This is also known as feline panleukopenia, feline distemper and feline parvovirus. The virus attacks the intestinal system. It is spread via the faeces and urine. The virus may survive for many years in some environments. The use of household bleach (sodium hypochlorite) for cleaning helps to prevent colonisation. Signs, among others, are diarrhoea, vomiting, depression, anorexia and dehydration. Death may occur within days. A vaccine is available from your vet.

FELINE VIRAL RHINOTRACHEITIS (FVR) & CALCIVIRUS (FCV)

Also known as cat flu, this is a complex of upper respiratory diseases. Signs are excessive hard sneezing, runny nose and mouth ulcers. Cats vaccinated after having contracted flu may recover but may suffer recurrent bouts, especially if they become stressed.

FELINE LEUKAEMIA VIRUS (FeLV)

This is an highly infectious viral disease. It is spread via direct contact—mutual grooming, saliva, feeding bowls, faeces, urine and biting. It can be passed prenatally

HEALTH AND VACCINATION SCHEDULE

AGE	6 WKS	8 WKS	10 WKS	12 WKS	16 WKS	6 MOS	1 YR
Worm control	✔	✔	✔		✔		
Neutering						✔	
Rhinotracheitis	✔	✔		✔	✔		✔
Panleukopenia	✔	✔		✔			✔
Calcivirus		✔			✔		✔
Feline Leukaemia				✔			✔
Feline Infectious Peritonitis				✔	✔		✔
Faecal evaluation						✔	
Feline Immunodeficiency testing							✔
Feline Leukaemia testing				✔			✔
Dental evaluation		✔				✔	
Rabies				✔	✔		✔

Vaccinations are not instantly effective. It takes about two weeks for the cat's immune system to develop antibodies. Most vaccinations require annual booster shots. Your veterinary surgeon should guide you in this regard.

DISEASE REFERENCE CHART

	What is it?	Cause	Symptoms
Feline Leukaemia Virus (FeLV)	Infectious disease; kills more cats each year than any other feline infectious disease.	A virus spread through saliva, tears, urine and faeces of infected cats; bite wounds.	Early on no symptoms may occur, but eventually infected cats experience signs from depression and weight loss to respiratory distress. FeLV also suppresses immune system, making a cat susceptible to almost any severe chronic illness.
Rabies	Potentially deadly virus that infects warm-blooded mammals.	A bacterium, often carried by rodents, that enters through mucous membranes and spreads quickly throughout the body.	Aggressiveness, a blank or vacant look in the eyes, increased vocalisation and/or weak or wobbly gait.
Feline Infectious Enteritis (FIE) *aka Panleukopenia*	Highly contagious virus, potentially deadly.	Ingestion of the virus, which is usually spread through the faeces of infected cats.	Most common: severe diarrhoea. Also vomiting, fatigue, lack of appetite, severe inflammation of intestines.
Feline Viral Rhinotracheitis (FVR)	Viral disease that affects eyes and upper respiratory tracts.	A virus that can affect any cat, especially those in multiple-cat settings.	Sneezing attacks, coughing, drooling thick saliva, fever, watery eyes, ulcers of mouth, nose and eyes.
Feline Immuno-deficiency Virus (FIV)	Virus that reduces white blood cells.	An infection spread commonly through cat-fight wounds.	Signs may be dormant for years or innocuous, such as diarrhoea or anaemia.
Feline Infectious Peritonitis (FIP)	A fatal viral disease, may be linked to FeLV and FIV.	Bacteria in dirty litter boxes; stress may increase susceptibility in kittens.	Extremely variable; range from abdominal swelling to chest problems, eye ailments and body lesions.
Feline Urological Syndrome (FUS)	A disease that affects the urinary tracts of cats.	Inflammation of bladder and urethra.	Constipation, constant licking of penis or vulva, blood in urine (males), swollen abdomen, crying when lifted.

from a female to her offspring. It creates tumours, anaemia, immune system depression, pyrexia (high temperatures), lethargy, respiratory disease, intestinal disease and many other potentially fatal problems. It is most prevalent in high-density cat populations. Not all cats will be affected, but they may become carriers.

Kittens less than six months old are especially vulnerable. Infected cats usually die by the time they are three to four years old. Cats can be screened or tested for this disease. Vaccination is not 100% effective but is recommended in kittens being sold into multi-cat environments.

FELINE IMMUNODEFICIENCY VIRUS (FIV)

This causes the white blood cells to be significantly reduced, thus greatly suppressing the efficiency of the immune system. It is not transferable to humans. Infection is normally gained from cat-fight wounds; thus, outdoor males are at the most risk. A cat diagnosed via blood tests as FIV-positive may live a normal life for months or years if retained indoors and given careful attention. Signs may be innocuous in the early stages, such as anaemia or diarrhoea. No vaccine is available.

FELINE INFECTIOUS PERITONITIS (FIP)
This viral disease is invariably fatal once contracted in its more potent forms. However, the virulence of the virus is variable and may by destroyed by the immune system. Stress may increase susceptibility in kittens. It may be linked to FeLV and FIV. Signs are extremely variable and range from abdominal swelling to chest problems, eye ailments to body lesions. There are various tests available but none is as yet 100% conclusive. Strict cleanliness is essential, especially of litter trays. No vaccine is available.

FELINE UROLOGICAL SYNDROME (FUS)
This is a very distressing condition caused by an inflammation of the bladder and urethra. Signs are constipation-like squatting and attempts to urinate, regular licking of the penis or vulva, blood in urine (males), swollen abdomen, crying when lifted and urinating in unusual places (often in only small amounts).

The numerous causes include infection, dirty litter tray of the indoor cat, alkaline urine (in cats it should be acidic), diet too dry, poor water intake (even though this may be available) and being hit by a vehicle (damaged nerves). Veterinary treatment is essential or the condition could be fatal due to the bladder bursting or the presence of dangerous bacteria.

RABIES
Currently Britain and most European Community countries are free of this terrible disease. The stringent quarantine laws of Britain are such that vaccination

STRESS TEST
Stress reduces the effectiveness of the immune system. Seemingly innocuous conditions may develop into major problems or leave the cat more open to attack by disease. Stress is difficult to specifically identify, but its major causes are well known. These include incorrect diet, intrusion by another cat in its home or territory, excessive handling and petting, disturbed sleep, uncomfortable home temperatures, bullying by another cat or pet, parasitic infestation, boarding in a cattery, travel, moving, boredom, limited accommodation space and, for some felines, being exhibited.

NEUTERING

Neutering is a major means of avoiding ill health. It dramatically reduces the risk of males' becoming involved in territorial battles with the dangers of physical injury and disease transference. It makes the male more placid and less likely to scent mark its home. It also reduces the incidence of prostate problems, and there is no risk of testicular cancer. The female avoids potentially lethal illnesses related to her being allowed to remain in an unmated condition, such as breast cancer.

Neutering is usually performed between four and six months of age, but it can be done as early as eight weeks of age. Data available on the age at which a kitten is neutered indicate that early neutering has more advantages than drawbacks. Breeders should have this performed on all cats sold as pets.

Male cats are neutered. The operation removes the testicles and requires that the cat be anaesthetised. Females are spayed. This is major surgery during which the ovaries and uterus are removed. Both males and females should be kept quiet at home for about seven to ten days following the procedure, at which time the vet will remove the sutures.

return to the UK without being placed into quarantine. The vaccination is given when the kitten is three or more months old. The pet passport process takes at least six months to complete, so plan well ahead.

COMMON HEALTH PROBLEMS

DERMATITIS (ECZEMA)

Dry, lifeless coat, loss of coat, tiny scabs over the head and body, loose flakes (dandruff) and excessive scratching are all commonly called eczema. The cause covers a range of possibilities including diet, parasitic mites such as *Cheyletiella spp*, fungus or an allergy to flea or other bites. Sometimes reasons are unknown. Veterinary diagnosis and treatment are required.

Sometimes an itch is just an itch!

has not been necessary. However, the introduction of passports for dogs and cats means that resident British cats must be vaccinated if they are to travel abroad and

RINGWORM (*DERMATOPHYTOSIS*)
This problem is fungal, not that of a worm. The most common form is *Microsporum canis*, which accounts for over 90% of cases. Cats less than one year old are at the highest risk, while longhaired cats are more prone to the problem than shorthaired cats. The fungi feed on the keratin layers of the skin, nails and hair. Direct contact and spores that remain in the environment are the main means of transmission.

Typical signs are circular-type bald areas of skin, which may be flaked and reddish. The coat generally may become dry and lifeless, giving the appearance of numerous other skin and hair problems. Veterinary diagnosis and treatment, either topical or via drugs, are essential as the condition is zoonotic, meaning that it can be transferred to humans.

THE RIB CAGE
Cats usually have 13 pairs of ribs. The ribs in the middle are longer than the ribs on either end (or beginning) of the rib cage. The first nine ribs are joined to the chest bone (sternum) with costal cartilages. Ribs 10, 11 and 12 are also associated with cartilage, which contributes to the costal arch. The thirteenth rib is called the floating rib and its cartilage is separate from the other ribs.

POSSIBLE SOURCES OF EAR PROBLEMS
• Fight scratches
• Excess secretion of wax
• Swellings and blood blisters (haematoma) resulting from intrusion by foreign bodies (grass seeds, etc.)
• Sunburn
• Whitish-coloured ear mites (*Otodectes cynotis*)
• Orange-coloured harvest mites (*Trombicula autumnalis*)
• Fleas
• Bacterial infection of either the outer or middle/inner ear

EAR PROBLEMS
Most of the common ear problems affect the outer ear. The telltale sign is the cat's constant scratching of the ears and/or its holding the ear to one side. Greasy hairs around the ear, dark brown wax (cerumen) in the ears, scaly flakes in or around the ear or minute white or orange pinhead-like bodies (mites) in the ear are common signs. Canker is a term used for ear infections, but it has no specific meaning.

Over-the-counter remedies for ear problems are usually ineffective unless correct diagnosis has been made. It is therefore better to let the vet diagnose and treat the cat. Some problems may require anaesthesia and minor surgery.

DIARRHOEA

This is a general term used to indicate a semi-liquid to liquid state of faecal matter. Mild to acute cases may be due to a change of environment, dietary change, eating an 'off' item, gorging on a favoured food, stress or a minor chill. These often rectify themselves within days. Chronic and persistent diarrhoea may be the result of a specific disease. Any indication of blood in the faecal matter must be considered dangerous.

In minor cases, withholding food for 12–24 hours, or feeding a simple diet, may arrest the condition. If not, contact your vet. Faecal analysis and blood testing may be required. By answering numerous questions related to the cat's diet, general health, level of activity, loss of appetite, etc., the vet will determine whether tests are required or if immediate treatment is warranted. Do not give cats human or canine

A DELICATE HEART

A cat's heart is as delicate as a human's heart, but it is much smaller. At full maturity, a queen's heart weighs between 9–12 grammes. The tom's heart is heavier, weighing 11–18 grammes. The blood that circulates through the heart chambers does not supply the heart muscle, thus requiring a separate circulatory system for the heart muscle.

CARE OF FELINE KIDNEYS

The kidney of the cat is larger than that of the dog, but it has the typical bean shape. It receives 25% of the blood output of the heart! For this reason, it has rather significant veins to accommodate this large supply of blood, and injuries suffered by the kidneys are usually serious and not uncommon.

intestinal remedies; these could prove dangerous.

CONSTIPATION

When a cat strains but is unable to pass motions, this is indicative of various causes. It may have hairballs, may have eaten a bird or rodent and has a bone lodged in its intestinal tract, may be suffering from a urological problem rather than constipation, or may have been hit by a car and has damaged the nerves that control bowel movements. As constipation is potentially serious, veterinary advice should be sought. Laxatives and faecal softener tablets may be given, the faecal matter can be surgically removed or another treatment carried out.

EXTERNAL PARASITES

FLEAS

Of all the problems to which cats are prone, none is more well known and frustrating than fleas. Indeed, flea-related problems are the principal cause of visits to veterinary surgeons. Flea infestation is relatively simple to cure but difficult to prevent. Periodic flea checks for your cat, conducted as well as annual health check-ups, are highly recommended. Consistent dosing with anthelmintic preparations is also advised. Parasites that are harboured inside the body are a bit more difficult to eradicate, but they are easier to control.

To control a flea infestation, you have to understand the flea's life cycle. Fleas are often thought of as a summertime problem but centrally heated homes have changed the life-cycle patterns, and fleas can be found at any time of the year. Fleas thrive in hot and humid environments; they soon die if the temperature drops below 2°C (35°F). The most effective method of flea control is a two-stage approach: one stage to kill the adult fleas, and the other to control the development of pre-adult fleas. Unfortunately, no single active ingredient is effective against all stages of the life cycle.

Flea prevention is a challenge to cat owners in most places. This is an adult male flea.

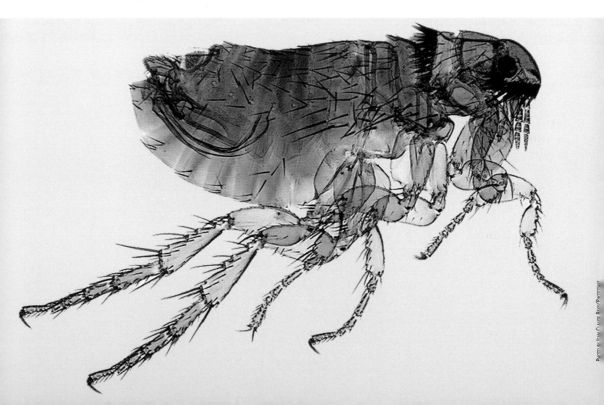

A Look at Fleas

Fleas have been around for millions of years and have adapted to changing host animals. They are able to go through a complete life cycle in less than one month, or they can extend their lives to almost two years by remaining as pupae or cocoons. They must have a blood meal every 10-14 days, and egg production begins within 2 days of their first meal. The female cat flea is very prolific and can lay 2000 eggs in her lifetime!

Fleas have been measured as being able to jump 300,000 times and can jump 150 times their body length in any direction, including straight up. Those are just a few of the reasons why they are so successful in infesting a cat!

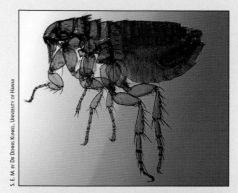

A scanning electron micrograph (S. E. M.) of a flea.

Magnified head of a flea.

LIFE CYCLE STAGES

During its life, a flea will pass through four life stages: egg, larva, pupa and adult. The adult stage is the most visible and irritating stage of the flea life cycle, and this is why the majority of flea-control products concentrate on this stage. The fact is that adult fleas account for only 1% of the total flea population, and the other 99% exist in pre-adult stages, i.e. eggs, larvae and pupae. The pre-adult stages are barely visible to the naked eye.

THE LIFE CYCLE OF THE FLEA

Eggs are laid on the cat, usually in quantities of about 20 or 30, several times a day. The female adult flea must have a blood meal before each egg-laying session. When first laid, the eggs will not cling to the cat's fur, as the eggs are not sticky. They will immediately fall to the floor or ground, especially when the cat moves around or scratches.

Once the eggs fall from the cat onto the carpet or grass, they will hatch into yellow larvae, approximately 2 mms long. This takes from 5 to 11 days. Larvae are not particularly mobile and will usually travel only a few inches from where they hatch. However, they do have a tendency to move away from light and heavy traffic—under furniture, in the carpet and behind doors are common places to find high quantities of flea larvae.

The flea larvae feed on dead organic matter, including adult flea faeces, until they are ready to change into adult fleas. Fleas will usually remain as larvae for around seven days, becoming darker in colour. After this period, the larvae will pupate a protective cocoon. While inside the pupae, the larvae will undergo metamorphosis and change into adult fleas. This can happen within a week, but the adult fleas can remain inside the pupae waiting to hatch for up to six months. The pupae are signalled to hatch by certain stimuli, such as physical pressure—the pupae's being stepped on, heat from an animal lying on the pupae or increased

Opposite page: A scanning electron micrograph of a flea, magnified more than 100x. This image has been colorized for effect.

DID YOU KNOW?
Never mix flea-control products without first consulting your veterinary surgeon. Some products can become toxic when combined with others and can cause serious or fatal consequences.

DID YOU KNOW?
Flea-killers are poisonous. You should not spray these toxic chemicals on areas of a cat's body that he licks, on his genitals or on his face. Flea killers taken internally are a better answer, but check with your vet in case internal therapy is not advised for your cat.

carbon dioxide levels and vibrations—indicating that a suitable host is available.

Once hatched, the adult flea must feed within a few days. Once the adult flea finds a host, it will not leave voluntarily. It only becomes dislodged by grooming or the host animal's scratching. The adult flea will remain on the host for the duration of its life unless forcibly removed.

TREATING THE ENVIRONMENT AND THE CAT

Treating fleas should be a two-pronged attack. First, the environment needs to be treated; this includes carpets and furniture, especially the cat's bedding and areas underneath furniture. The environment should be treated with a household spray containing an Insect Growth Regulator (IGR) and an insecticide to kill the adult fleas. There are also liquids, given orally, that contain chitin inhibitors. These

A brown tick, *Rhipicephalus sanguineus*, is an uncommon but annoying tick found on cats.

The head of a tick, *Dermacentor variabilis*, enlarged and coloured for effect.

Dwight R Kuhn's magnificent action photo, showing a flea jumping.

render flea eggs incapable of development. There are also both foam and liquid wipe-on treatments. Additionally, cats can be injected with treatments that can last up to six months. Emulsions that have the same effect can also be added to food. The advanced treatments are only available from veterinary surgeons. The IGRs actually mimic the fleas' own hormones and stop the eggs and larvae from developing into adult fleas. There are currently no treatments available to attack the pupa stage of the life cycle, so the adult insecticide is used to kill the newly hatched adult fleas before they find a host. Most IGRs are active for many months, while adult insecticides are only active for a few days.

When treating with a household spray, it is a good idea to vacuum before applying the product. This stimulates as many pupae as possible to hatch into adult fleas. The vacuum cleaner should also be treated with a flea

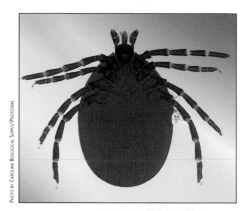

PHOTO BY CAROLINA BIOLOGICAL SUPPLY/PHOTOTAKE

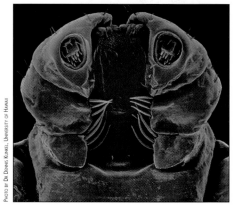

PHOTO BY DR DENNIS KUNKEL, UNIVERSITY OF HAWAII

treatment to prevent the eggs and larvae that have been hoovered into the vacuum bag from hatching.

The second stage of treatment is to apply an adult insecticide to the cat, usually in the form of a collar or a spray. Alternatively, there are drops that, when placed on the back of the animal's neck, spread throughout the fur and skin to kill adult fleas. A word of warning: Never use products sold for dogs on your cat; the result could be fatal.

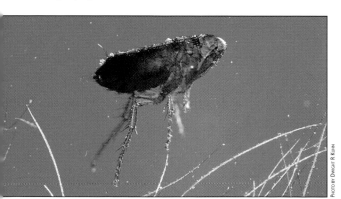

PHOTO BY DWIGHT R KUHN

The Life Cycle of the Flea

Eggs

Larvae

Pupa

Adult

Photos courtesy of Fleabusters®, Rx for Fleas.

Flea Control

IGR (INSECT GROWTH REGULATOR)

Two types of products should be used when treating fleas—a product to treat the pet and a product to treat the home. Adult fleas represent 1% of the flea population. The pre-adult fleas (eggs, larvae and pupae) represent 99% of the flea population and are found in the environment; it is in the case of pre-adult fleas that products containing an Insect Growth Regulator (IGR) should be used in the home.

IGRs are a new class of compounds used to prevent the development of insects. They do not kill the insect outright, but instead use the insect's biology against it to stop it from completing its growth. Products that contain methoprene are the world's first and leading IGRs. Used to control fleas and other insects, this type of IGR will stop flea larvae from developing and protect the house for up to seven months.

EN GARDE: CATCHING FLEAS OFF GUARD!

Consider the following ways to arm yourself against fleas:
• Add a small amount of pennyroyal or eucalyptus oil to your cat's bath. These natural remedies repel fleas.
• Supplement your cat's food with fresh garlic (minced or grated) and a hearty amount of brewer's yeast, both of which ward off fleas.
• Use a flea comb on your cat daily. Submerge fleas in a cup of bleach to kill them quickly.
• Confine the cat to only a few rooms to limit the spread of fleas in the home.
• Vacuum daily...and get all of the crevices! Dispose of the bag every few days until the problem is under control.
• Wash your cat's bedding daily. Cover cushions where your cat sleeps with towels, and wash the towels often.

TICKS AND MITES

Though not as common as fleas, ticks and mites are found all over the tropical and temperate world. They don't bite like fleas; they harpoon. They dig their sharp proboscis (nose) into the cat's skin and drink the blood. Their only food and drink is your cat's blood. Cats can get potentially fatal anaemia, paralysis and many other diseases from ticks and mites. They may live where fleas are found and they like to hide in cracks or seams in walls wherever cats live. They are controlled the same way fleas are controlled.

The *Dermacentor variabilis* may well be the most common tick in many geographical areas, especially those areas where the climate is hot and humid. The other common ticks that attack small animals are *Rhipicephalus sanguineus, Ixodes* and some species of *Amblyomma*.

Most ticks have life expectancies of a week to six months, depending upon climatic conditions. They can neither jump nor fly, but they can crawl slowly and can range up to 5 metres (16 feet) to reach a sleeping or unsuspecting animal.

INTERNAL PARASITES

Most animals—fishes, birds and mammals, including cats and humans—have worms and other parasites that live inside their bodies. According to Dr Herbert R

Axelrod, the fish pathologist, there are two kinds of parasites: dumb and smart. The smart parasites live in peaceful cooperation with their hosts (symbiosis), while the dumb parasites kill their hosts. Most of the worm infections are relatively

TOXOPLASMOSIS AND PREGNANT WOMEN

Toxoplasmosis is caused by a single parasite, *Toxoplasma gondii*. Cats acquire it by eating infected prey, such as rodents or birds, or raw meat. Obviously, strictly indoor cats are at less risk of infection than cats that are permitted to roam outdoors. Symptoms include diarrhoea, listlessness, pneumonia and inflammation of the eye. Sometimes there are no symptoms. The disease can be treated with antibiotics.

The only way humans can get the disease is through direct contact with the cat's faeces. People usually don't display any symptoms, although they can show mild flu-like symptoms. Once exposed, an antibody is produced and the person builds immunity to the disease.

The real danger to humans is that pregnant women can pass the parasite to the developing foetus. In this case the chances are good that the baby will be born with a major health problem and/or serious birth defects. In order to eliminate risk, pregnant women should have someone else deal with the litter-box duties or wear gloves while taking care of the litter box and wash hands thoroughly afterwards.

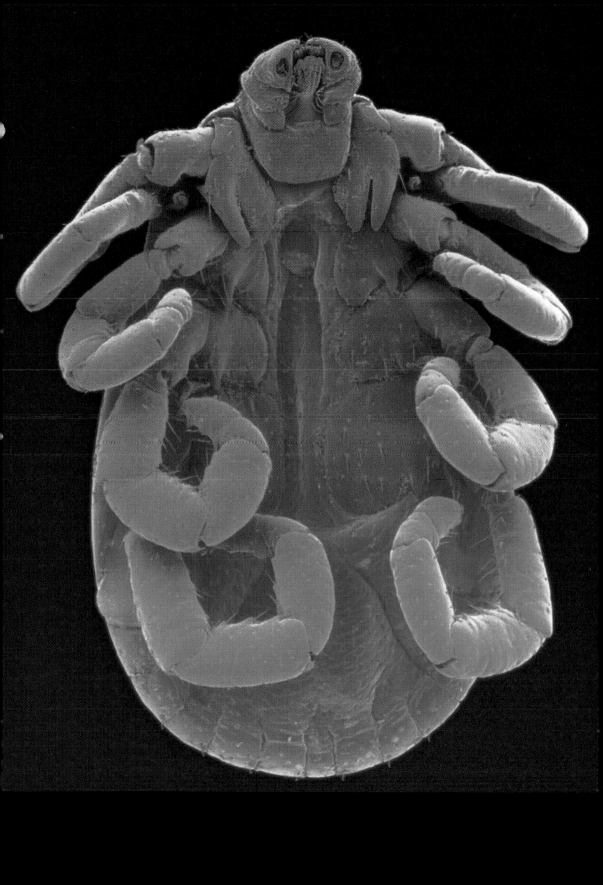

easy to control. If they are not controlled, they weaken the host cat to the point that other medical problems occur, but they are not dumb parasites.

HOOKWORMS

The worm *Ancylostoma tubaeforme* can infect a cat by larva penetrating its skin. It attaches itself to the small intestine of the cat, where it sucks blood. This loss of blood could cause iron-deficiency anaemia.

Outdoor cats that spend much of their time in the garden or in contact with soil are commonly infected with hookworm. There is another worm, the *Gordius* or a horsehair worm, that, if ingested by a cat, causes vomiting.

TAPEWORMS

There are many species of tapeworms. They are carried by

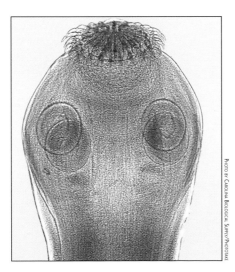

The head and rostellum (the round prominence on the scolex) of a tapeworm, which infects cats and humans.

PHOTO BY CAROLINA BIOLOGICAL SUPPLY/PHOTOTAKE

DEWORMING

Ridding your kitten of worms is VERY IMPORTANT because certain worms that kittens carry, such as tapeworms and roundworms, can infect humans.

Breeders initiate a deworming programme at or about four weeks of age. The routine is repeated every two or three weeks until the kitten is three months old. The breeder from whom you obtained your kitten should provide you with the complete details of the deworming programme.

Your veterinary surgeon can prescribe and monitor the programme of deworming for you. The usual programme is treating the kitten every 15–20 days until the kitten is positively worm-free.

It is advised that you only treat your kitten with drugs that are recommended professionally.

fleas! The cat eats the flea and starts the tapeworm cycle. Humans can also be infected with tapeworms, so don't eat fleas! Fleas are so small that your cat could pass them onto your hands, your plate or your food and thus make it possible for you to ingest a flea that is carrying tapeworm eggs.

While tapeworm infection is not life-threatening in cats (smart parasite!), it can be the cause of a

INTERNAL PARASITES OF CATS

NAME	DESCRIPTION	SYMPTOMS	ACQUISITION	TREATMENT
Roundworm (*Toxocara cati* and *Toxascaris leonina*)	Large, white, coil-like worms, 2–4 inches long, resembling small springs.	Vomiting, pot belly, respiratory problems, poor growth rate, protruding third eyelids, poor haircoat.	Ingesting infective larvae; ingesting infected mammals, birds or insects; a queen with *Toxocari cati* nursing kittens.	Anthelmintics; scrupulously clean environment (e.g. daily removal of all faeces recommended).
***Physaloptera* species**	1–6 inches long, attacks the wall of the stomach.	Vomiting, anorexia, melena.	Eating insects that live in soil (e.g. May beetles).	Diagnosed with a gastroscope; treated with pyrantel pamoate. Prevention of exposure to the intermediate hosts.
***Gordius* or Horsehair worm**	6-inch pale brown worms with stripes.	Vomiting.	May ingest a worm while drinking from or making contact with swimming pools and toilet bowls.	Anthelmintics; avoiding potentially infected environments.
Hookworm (*Ancylostoma tubaeforme*)	The adult worms, ranging from 6 to 15 mms in length, attach themselves to the small intestines.	Anaemia, melena, weight loss, poor haircoat.	Larva penetrating the cat's skin, usually attacks the small intestine. Found in soil and flower gardens where faecal matter is deposited.	Fortnightly treatment with anthelmintics. Good sanitation (e.g. daily cleanup of litter boxes).
Tapeworm (*Dipylidium caninum* and *Taenia taeniformis*)	Up to 3 feet long. Parts shaped similar to cucumber seeds. The most common intermediate hosts are fleas and biting lice.	No clinical signs—difficult to detect.	Eating infected adult fleas. Uses rodents as hosts.	Praziquantel and epsiprantel. Management of environment to ensure scrupulously clean conditions. Proper flea control.

Magnified heartworm larvae, *Dirofilaria immitis*.

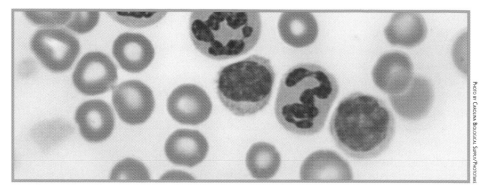

Photo by Carolina Biological Supply/Phototake

The heartworm, *Dirofilaria immitis*.

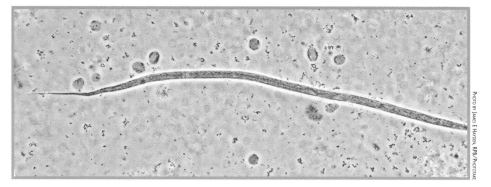

Photo by James E Hayden, RPB./Phototake

very serious liver disease for humans. About 50 percent of the humans infected with *Echinococcus multilocularis*, a type of tapeworm that causes alveolar hydatis, perish.

HEARTWORMS

Heartworms are thin, extended worms up to 30 cms (12 ins) long, which are difficult to diagnose in cats as the worms are too few to be identified by the antigen-detection test. Symptoms may be loss of energy, loss of appetite, coughing, the development of a pot belly and anaemia. Heartworm infection in cats should be treated very seriously, as it is often fatal.

Heartworms are transmitted by mosquitoes. The mosquito drinks the blood of an infected cat and takes in larvae with the blood. It takes two to three weeks for the larvae to develop to the infective stage within the body of the mosquito. Cats are less frequently infected with heartworms than dogs are. Also, the parasite is more likely to attack the cat's brain or other organs rather than the heart. Cats should be treated at about six weeks of age, and maintained on a prophylactic dose given monthly.

THE FELINE EYE

by Lorraine Waters BvetNed, CertVOphthal, MRCVS

This part of the book aims to provide an owner's guide to feline ophthalmology. Ophthalmology is the study of eyes.

Eye diseases in the cat usually result from trauma, infection or neoplasia. Unlike the dog, the cat has few inherited eye conditions. Most of the conditions to be discussed are not amenable to first-aid measures or home remedies. Therefore, if you are at all worried about your cat's eye, you should seek prompt veterinary attention.

Ocular pain is frequently associated with eye disease and can be recognised in your cat because it will show a combination of the following signs: blinking, increased tear production, fear of light and rubbing at the eye. Some conditions result in loss of vision; a gradual loss of vision may go unnoticed, as the cat slowly adapts, but a sudden loss produces an obvious change in behaviour. Being blind may not be as bad as it sounds, as cats adapt and cope amazingly well in familiar surroundings.

To examine the eye properly, veterinary surgeons first use a bright light, which allows close examination of the lids, conjunctiva, cornea and iris. Following this, an ophthalmoscope can be used, in a darkened room, to give a magnified view. Then by using the lenses within the ophthalmoscope, it is possible to focus on the structures further back in the eye, such as the lens, vitreous and retina.

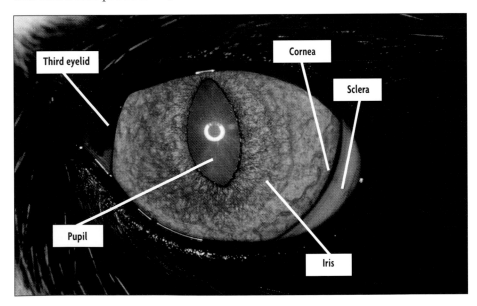

Third eyelid

Cornea

Sclera

Pupil

Iris

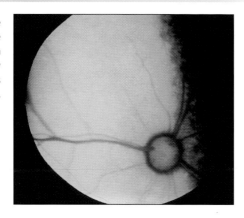

The feline fundus, the eye as seen through the veterinary surgeon's ophthalmoscope.

DISEASES OF THE FELINE EYE

GLOBE AND ORBIT

The eye sits in a bony socket in the skull known as the orbit. In short-nosed breeds, the orbit is shallow and the normal-sized eyes bulge forward. This situation can predispose a number of problems, such as exposure keratitis, overflow of tears and even prolapse of the globe (eye). Cats can be born with eyes that are too small and sink back into the orbit, to be covered by the third eyelid. This is non-inherited and usually associated with damage to the eye in utero. Abnormal enlargement of the globe may be congenital (buphthalmos) or acquired (hydrophthalmos) and is the end point of glaucoma.

The globe can prolapse from the orbit following head trauma, a common injury for cats involved in road traffic accidents. A minor prolapse replaced early can result in restoration of normal function. However, there is often stretching of the optic nerve and tearing of the extra-ocular muscles. In these cases, the eye may be permanently damaged and have to be surgically removed. As an emergency measure, applying a moist cloth to the prolapsed eye on the way to the surgery will help preserve it.

Problems behind the eye become evident when they cause the eye to bulge forward along with the third eyelid. These include tooth root abscesses, foreign bodies, tumours and occasionally haemorrhage.

EYELIDS

The eyes of a kitten should open around 10–14 days of age. Once this has occurred, it is possible to see if the lids have been properly formed. Failure of all or part of the eyelids to develop is a rare congen-

EYE DROPS

Topical ointments and drops are often prescribed for the treatment of eye disease. There are a few simple rules to follow when administering them. It is important to clean away discharges before applying treatment. Only give one drop or just a few millimetres of ointment; if you give too much, it will be diluted by increased tear production. Systemic drugs are those given by mouth to achieve higher concentrations at the back of the eye or for diseases which involve other body systems.

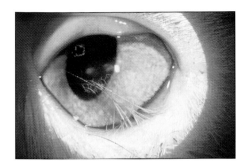

ital problem, known as coloboma. The unprotected cornea, in the affected area, may become damaged and the lid must be surgically restored. Early infection in the eye may delay or prevent eyelid opening; the lids can be opened surgically to allow bathing and appropriate medication to be given.

Entropion and ectropion are common conditions in the dog and are related to conformation. Fortunately these are rare in cats and can be surgically corrected. Entropion secondary to ocular pain may remain once the cause of the pain is removed. Fortunately, these cases will respond to corrective surgery. Extra or abnormally positioned hairs are frequently seen as an inherited problem in dogs, but are rare in cats.

There are several types of tumours that can occur on the eyelids. The most common type is squamous cell carcinoma, more prevalent in white and part-white cats, as ultra-violet light (sunlight) plays a role in causing this condition. Treatment may consist

of cryotherapy, surgical excision or radiation treatment. Early recognition and treatment is essential to prevent destructive local spreading.

Eyelid coloboma is a rare congenital problem in cats.

CONJUNCTIVA

The pink tissue lining the eyelid and covering the third eyelid and front of the sclera is called conjunctiva. Dermoids are elements of skin tissue that arise in abnormal places. Dermoids often, but not invariably, contain hairs and can form on the conjunctiva and/or cornea. Dermoids act as foreign bodies in the eye, causing irritation and pain, and need to be surgically removed.

The most frequently encountered problem with the conjunctiva is conjunctivitis. In cats, the majority of cases are infectious. An eye with conjunctivitis usually looks red and swollen with signs of ocular pain. Discharges may be watery or sticky yellow, indicating bacterial infection.

The most common infectious cause of feline conjunctivitis is feline herpesvirus (FHV). Feline calicivirus (FCV) can also cause

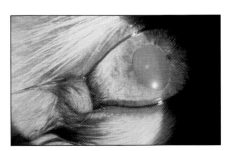

Dermoid in a longhaired cat.

Conjunctivitis, frequently an infectious disease in cats.

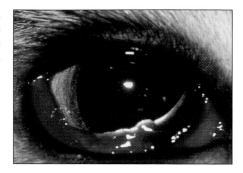

Corneal ulcer stained with fluorescein.

conjunctivitis and is usually associated with other problems, such as upper respiratory tract problems and mouth ulcers. The bacteria *Chlamydia psittaci* can cause conjunctivitis in individual cats and in a multi-cat households. Individual cases respond well to appropriate antibiotic therapy. Chronic and recurrent conjunctivitis in multi-cat situations requires thorough and prolonged treatment, management changes and, where appropriate, vaccination. *Mycoplasma spp.* can cause a less severe conjunctivitis then *Chlamydia spp.* Opportunistic infection can occur following cat-fight wounds, as bacteria are found on cats' teeth and claws.

Tear staining is more commonly seen in short-nosed cat breeds.

Non-infectious causes of conjunctivitis include trauma, foreign bodies, allergic disease, tumours and pre-corneal tear film abnormalities. Eosinophilic kerato-conjunctivitis is a disease where the conjunctiva and cornea are invaded by cells from the immune system, primarily mast cells and eosinophils. These cells are responsible for inflammation and allergic reactions. This tends to occur in young to middle-aged cats and may

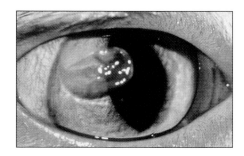

be seasonal. Treatment usually works well but may be required long-term.

Several forms of neoplasia (cancer) can affect the conjunctiva in cats and can be either primary tumours, arising in the conjunctiva, or secondary, spreading from elsewhere in the body.

SCLERA
The sclera is the white fibrous coat of the globe. It is partially covered by conjunctiva and protects the more fragile internal structures. Congenital defects of this structure are very rare. Inflammation

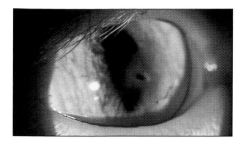

(scleritis and episcleritis) is a problem in dogs and humans but is extremely rare in cats. Feline scleral diseases are usually associated with trauma and neoplasia.

PRE-CORNEAL TEAR FILM

This forms from tears and moistens, lubricates and helps protect the cornea. Decreased tear production occurs if the tear glands are not working properly and results in a condition called 'dry eye' or keratoconjunctivis sicca (KCS). The cornea becomes dry and roughened leading to keratitis and ulceration. It can occur following feline herpesvirus (FHV) infection, trauma, facial paralysis and chronic inflammation.

Overproduction of tears can be seen as a result of ocular pain. The naso-lacrimal duct drains the tears; it runs from the inner corner of the eye to just inside the end of the nose. Congenital defects, such as a small duct opening, result in tear overflow and staining around the eye. These can usually be corrected surgically. Acquired blockages may result from chronic conjunctivitis or foreign bodies.

Tear staining is also seen in short-nosed breeds because the duct is tortuous and drainage inadequate. This is also associated with medial lower lid entropion, occluding the duct opening. This anatomical combination is very difficult to improve surgically.

Corneal foreign body.

CORNEA

The cornea is the clear circular area at the front of the eye through which the iris and pupil can be seen. Light passes through and is focused by the cornea, before passing through the lens and hence onto the retina. Congenital defects are rare but include micro- and megalocornea. There is sometimes a transient cloudiness following opening of the eyes but it should disappear by four weeks of age.

One of the most common problems involving the cornea is ulceration, where the top layer of corneal cells (the epithelium) is lost and the nerve endings exposed, resulting in ocular pain. Fluorescein is a special stain that can be used to demonstrate ulcers;

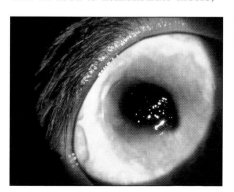

Corneal sequestrum.

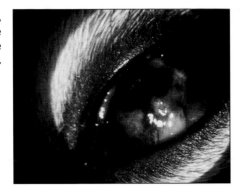

Symblepharon, adhesion of the eyelid to the eyeball.

they show up as a yellow/green patch on the cornea. If your cat has had this performed, you may have noticed the stain appearing at the end of its nose; this is because it drains down the naso-lacrimal duct and demonstrates that it is not blocked.

The most common cause of ulceration is trauma, from fight wounds or foreign bodies. FHV can cause ulceration. There is also a form of ulceration where the epithelium does not stick down again after healing and can easily become detached. This is seen as a breed-related problem in dogs. In cats it can be seen in older animals or associated with FHV infection, resulting in recurrent ulcer formation.

The cornea is very quick to repair ulcers and, provided that the initial cause is removed, healing should only take a few days. Antibiotics are often applied to the eye while ulcers heal to prevent bacterial infection. Ulcers need prompt veterinary attention as they

can deteriorate rapidly; deep ulcers can lead to rupture of the eye and require urgent surgical repair.

The cornea is a common site for cat scratch injuries and some may even penetrate the full thickness into the anterior chamber. If these wounds are repaired quickly and appropriate medical therapy is used, vision can usually be preserved. More severe ones may require reconstructive surgery, removal of the lens or even surgical removal of the eye.

Corneal foreign bodies usually result in ocular pain and need to be removed. Non-painful ones also need to be removed as they may penetrate the eye, causing internal problems.

Corneal sequestrum or necrosis is a condition specific to cats. The corneal stroma (middle layer) degenerates, turns brown/black and emerges through the epithelium, causing ulceration and a foreign body reaction with signs of ocular pain. These lesions usually need to be removed surgically because of the discomfort they cause, but a few will slough off naturally. Often a sequestrum will recur in the same eye or occur in the opposite eye at a later date. This condition is most commonly seen in Colourpoint Persians and is thought to have an inherited component. It may be related to their prominent eye position. The next most common breed with sequestra is the Burmese.

Following healing of a corneal wound, there is usually formation of a scar, which shows up as a white mark. Unless they are extensive, they do not usually affect vision.

FHV-RELATED EYE DISEASES

A combination of treatments is often required to treat feline herpesvirus (FHV) infection. In acute cases, kittens are often very sick and need supportive treatment and intensive nursing. Systemic and topical antibiotics are used, sometimes in combination with topical antiviral drugs. Cats that develop symblepharon after acute infection may be blinded by the condition and require new reconstructive surgical techniques. The chronic cases can be difficult to diagnose and challenging to treat. Topical antivirals can be used and, in non-ulcerated cases, combined with corticosteroids. More recent treatments include L-lysine (to inhibit viral replication), Cimetidine and interferon (to boost the local immune response).

The reason for chronic FHV disease is that individuals become carriers of the virus. When they are stressed, the virus is reactivated and signs of infection and the cat's immune response to it manifest in the eye. This can be a major problem in multi-cat households with carrier animals infecting kittens and adults alike. In these cases, management changes, including the identification of carriers, use of early vaccinations and isolation of new arrivals, must be instituted.

AQUEOUS HUMOUR

The aqueous humour is a watery fluid that is responsible for maintaining pressure within the eye. If the drainage angle is blocked and aqueous cannot drain away, pressure within the eye builds up, causing glaucoma. Glaucoma due to a congenitally obstructed drainage system is an inherited problem in many breeds of dog but is rare in the cat. When glaucoma does occur in cats, it is usually acquired, with drainage blocked by inflammatory or neoplastic cells.

Anterior uveitis can result in white blood cells in the anterior chamber, which gives it a cloudy look known as aqueous flare. Infection following penetrating wounds can result in pus accumulating in the chamber, known as hypopyon. Trauma to the eye and intra-ocular tumours may lead to bleeding into the anterior chamber (space behind the cornea and in

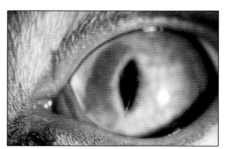

Herpesvirus ulcer.

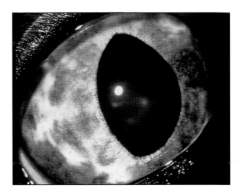

front of the iris), known as hyphaema. This blood usually forms a clot and is absorbed. Foreign bodies can also occasionally be seen in the anterior chamber.

IRIS AND CILIARY BODY

The iris and ciliary body are muscular and vascular structures, which lie behind the cornea and in front of the lens. The iris is pigmented and gives the cat's eye its colour. Congenital defects are rare, but occasionally cats are born with pieces of the iris missing. Changes in iris colour can occur for a number of reasons; as young cats mature, their iris colour may deepen. Inflammation results in reddening of the iris, due to an increase in blood vessel formation and engorgement, and is known as rubeosis iridis. Following inflammation, the iris can remain permanently dark. As cats age, they can develop a condition called melanosis. This is usually but not always a diffuse change, occurring

slowly in both eyes. It must be monitored and differentiated from iris melanoma. Melanoma is a tumour of the pigment cells that can result in either diffuse or nodular discoloration of the iris. It usually progresses quickly and only in one eye. This type of neoplasia has a potential to spread outside the eye and is usually treated by surgically removing the affected eye.

A difference in colour between the two irises is known as heterochromia iridis and can occur naturally in white or poorly pigmented breeds, usually associated with congenital deafness. In other cats, it usually indicates a problem in one eye or the other.

The ciliary body and iris are known as the anterior uvea, while the choroid (the vascular layer that lies between the retina and the sclera and provides a blood supply to the retina) is the posterior uvea. Uveitis is an inflammation of the uvea. It may involve both the anterior and posterior uvea and has

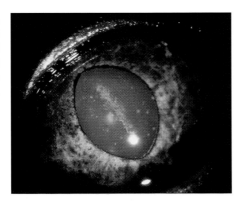

Iris melanoma, exhibited as a tumour of pigment cells that results in discoloration of the iris.

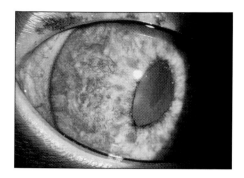

many causes in the cat. The main infectious causes are feline immunodeficiency virus (FIV), feline leukaemia virus (FeLV), feline infectious peritonitis (FIP) and toxoplasmosis. Tuberculosis has been reported in cats as a cause of uveitis, and in sub-tropical and tropical countries fungal infection can be a significant cause. The signs of uveitis for all these diseases are very similar and may include a constricted pupil, rubeosis iridis, aqueous flare, poor vision and ocular pain. It can be difficult to determine the cause in some cases despite thorough investigation. Even if the primary viral infection cannot be cured, cats with uveitis can be treated symptomatically to ease discomfort and maintain vision. Long-term uveitis can lead to cataract formation, lens luxation and glaucoma. Non-infectious causes of uveitis include trauma and neoplasia.

Atrophy of the iris may occur as a result of ageing or following inflammation. Cysts of the iris are sometimes seen and look like black balloons. They form on the back of the iris but can detach and float through the pupil to rest in front. They are not neoplastic and do not usually need to be removed.

Uveitis, inflammation of the iris, ciliary body and choroid.

LENS

The lens is the clear disc-shaped structure suspended behind the iris and is responsible for focusing light onto the retina. A cataract, or opacity of the lens and/or its capsule, is a disorder of the lens. Many forms of hereditary cataract are seen in dogs but not in cats. Congenital cataracts are occasionally found as a non-inherited problem. Most of the cataracts seen in cats are formed secondary to lens damage, e.g. blunt trauma, penetrating wounds, chronic anterior uveitis and lens luxation. If cataracts involve the whole lens, light will not be able to get through to the retina and the eye will be rendered blind. If appropriate, cataracts can be surgically removed.

If the lens's suspensory fibres weaken or break, it will become dislocated and can fall either into the back or front of the eye. This is

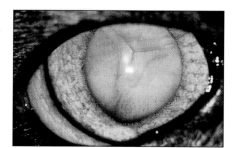

Cataract developed from long-term uveitis.

a common breed-related problem in terrier dogs and is occasionally seen in cats, usually as a result of trauma, ageing or cataract. The lens is usually surgically removed to prevent it from blocking the pupil, which can lead to glaucoma.

The lens condenses with age, giving it a grey appearance, known as senile sclerosis. This is not a true cataract as light can still pass through to the back of the eye and vision is not impaired.

One rare but important condition of the lens in the cat is post-traumatic sarcoma. If the lens is damaged by trauma, it can become neoplastic and rapidly fill the eye with tumours. Appropriate treatment at the time of the initial injury should prevent this, but when it does occur, surgical removal of the eye is recommended.

VITREOUS HUMOUR

The vitreous humour is a jelly-like substance that fills the space between the back of the lens and the front of the retina. Like the aqueous humour, the vitreous can be infiltrated with haemorrhage and inflammatory cells. Foreign bodies can occasionally be found in the vitreous. Inflammation of the vitreous, known as hyalitis, can be seen as part of generalised uveitis.

The vitreous humour degenerates with age, giving a cloudy appearance to the back of the eye,

> **THINGS TO LOOK OUT FOR**
> A change in appearance of the eye
> - Redness
> - Cloudiness
> - Change in iris colour
>
> Increase in discharges
> - Watery
>
> Sticky mucoid
> - Yellow
> - Bloody
>
> Blinking, squinting and head shyness
> Aversion to light
> Rubbing at the eye
> Loss of vision
> Protrusion of the eye
> Loss of facial symmetry

but this does not usually affect vision to any great extent.

RETINA

The retina, at the back of the eye, is where the visual image is formed. Congenital retinal problems are rare in cats, but colobomas (defects or holes) can occasionally be seen in the optic disc (the point at which nerves converge to leave the eye as the optic nerve). Inflammation of the retina usually occurs together with inflammation of the choroid and is called chorioretinitis or posterior uveitis. The causes are the same as those for anterior uveitis. Inflammation can lead to retinal detachment, haemorrhage, degeneration and scarring of the retina. It can be difficult to diagnose the cause of

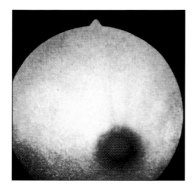

posterior uveitis; symptomatic treatment is generally given to maintain vision.

The retina may also degenerate as a result of non-inflammatory processes. An inherited form of retinal degeneration has been described in the Abyssinian and Siamese breeds. Deficiency in dietary taurine (an amino acid) causes retinal degeneration. Fortunately, this is now rare, as proprietary cat foods are supplemented with this compound. It may, however, still be a problem with some home-prepared diets.

Hypertension is a common cause of retinal disease in elderly cats. It may be primary essential hypertension or secondary to other diseases, such as kidney disease, hyperthyroidism and diabetes. Hypertension causes changes in the retinal arteries, retinal and vitreal haemorrhages, retinal detachment and hyphaema. Early recognition and treatment are essential to prevent permanent ocular damage and damage to other organs, such as the kidney, heart and brain.

Retinal detachment causes blindness and may result from hypertension, inflammation and neoplasia. If the retina does not reattach in 24–48 hours, there will be permanent vision loss. Symptomatic treatment is often given to reattach the retina, but it is also important to treat the underlying cause.

Retinal haemorrhages can occur as a result of hypertension, inflammation and trauma. They can cause temporary loss of vision but will often be resorbed. Once again, it is important to find the underlying cause and treat it accordingly without delay.

Finally, if in any doubt regarding the condition of your cat's eyes, it is always worthwhile consulting your veterinary surgeon. Even if you consider the condition minor, it may not remain so!

Advanced retinal degeneration.

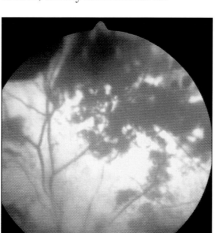

Retinal haemorrhages as a result of hypertension.

The author is grateful to the Animal Health Trust (England) for the illustrations used in the eye health section.

THE GERIATRIC CAT

Depending on lifestyle, most cats are considered old at 12 years of age. Some problems that are associated with cats in their senior years are:

- Decreased energy
- Intolerance to heat and cold
- Less meticulous grooming and litter-box habits
- Decrease in mental alertness
- Decline of liver and kidney functions
- Greater susceptibility to diseases, especially dental disease
- Increased occurrence of cancer

As long as owners pay attention and adjust for changing behaviour and diet and continue regular veterinary care, cats can live well into their teens—some even 20 years and older!

WHAT TO DO WHEN THE TIME COMES

You are never fully prepared to make a rational decision about putting your cat to sleep. It is very obvious that you love your Manx or you would not be reading this book. Putting a loved cat to sleep is extremely difficult. It is a decision that must be made with your veterinary surgeon. You are usually forced to make the decision when your beloved pet will only suffer more and experience no enjoyment for the balance of its life. Then euthanasia is the right choice.

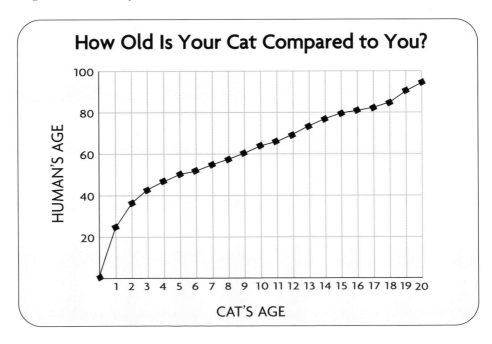

How Old Is Your Cat Compared to You?

HUMAN'S AGE

CAT'S AGE

WHAT IS EUTHANASIA?

Euthanasia derives from the Greek, meaning *good death.* In other words, it means the planned, painless killing of a cat suffering from a painful, incurable condition, or who is so aged that it cannot walk, see, eat or control its excretory functions.

Euthanasia is usually accomplished by injection with an overdose of an anaesthesia or barbiturate. Aside from the prick of the needle, the experience is usually painless.

MAKING THE DECISION

The decision to euthanise your cat is never easy. The days during which the cat becomes ill and the end occurs can be unusually stressful for you. If this is your first experience with the death of a loved one, you may need the comfort dictated by your religious beliefs. If you are the head of the family and have children, you should have involved them in the decision of putting your Manx to sleep. Usually your cat can be maintained on drugs for a few days in order to give you ample time to make a decision. During this time, talking with members of your family or even people who have lived through this same experience can ease the burden of your inevitable decision.

THE FINAL RESTING PLACE

Cats can have some of the same privileges as humans. The remains of your beloved cat can be buried in a pet cemetery, which is generally expensive. Cats who have died at home can be buried in your garden in a place suitably marked with some stone or newly planted tree or bush. Alternatively, they can be cremated individually and the ashes returned to you. A less expensive option is mass cremation, although, of course, the ashes cannot then be returned. Vets can usually arrange the cremation on your behalf. The cost of these options should always be discussed frankly and openly with your veterinary surgeon.

The remains of your beloved Manx can be buried in a pet cemetery.

HOMEOPATHY:
an alternative to conventional medicine

'Less is Most'

Using this principle, the strength of a homeopathic remedy is measured by the number of serial dilutions that were undertaken to create it. The greater the number of serial dilutions, the greater the strength of the homeopathic remedy. The potency of a remedy that has been made by making a dilution of 1 part in 100 parts (or 1/100) is 1c or 1cH. If this remedy is subjected to a series of further dilutions, each one being 1/100, a more dilute and stronger remedy is produced. If the remedy is diluted in this way six times, it is called 6c or 6cH. A dilution of 6c is 1 part in 1000,000,000,000. In general, higher potencies in more frequent doses are better for acute symptoms and lower potencies in more infrequent doses are more useful for chronic, long-standing problems.

CURING OUR CATS NATURALLY
Holistic medicine means treating the *whole* animal as a unique, perfect living being. Generally, holistic treatments do not suppress the symptoms that the body naturally produces, as do most medications prescribed by conventional doctors and vets. Holistic methods seek to cure disease by regaining balance and harmony in the patient's environment. Some of these methods include use of nutritional therapy, herbs, flower essences, aromatherapy, acupuncture, massage, chiropractic and, of course, the most popular holistic approach, homeopathy. Homeopathy is a theory or system of treating illness with small doses of substances which, if administered in larger quantities, would produce the symptoms that the patient already has. This approach is often described as 'like cures like.' Although modern veterinary medicine is geared toward the 'quick fix,' homeopathy relies on the belief that, given the time, the body is able to heal itself and return to its natural, healthy state.

Choosing a remedy to cure a problem in our cats is the difficult part of homeopathy. Consult with your veterinary surgeon for a professional diagnosis of your cat's symptoms. Often these symptoms require immediate conventional care. If your vet is willing, and somewhat knowledgeable, you may attempt a homeopathic remedy. Be aware that cortisone prevents homeopathic remedies from working. There are hundreds of possibilities and combinations to cure many problems in cats, from basic physical problems such as excessive moulting, fleas or other parasites, fever, severe skin problems, obesity, upset tummy, dry, oily or dull coat, diarrhoea, ear problems or eye discharge (including tears and dry or mucousy matter), to behavioural abnormalities, such as fear of loud noises, hypersensitivity to pain, poor appetite, aversion to touch and various phobias. From alumina to zincum metallicum, the remedies span the planet and the imagination...from flowers and weeds to chemicals, insect droppings, table salt and volcanic ash.

Using 'Like to Treat Like'

Unlike conventional medicines that suppress symptoms, homeopathic remedies treat illnesses with small doses of substances that, if administered in larger quantities, would produce the symptoms that the patient already has. While the same homeopathic remedy can be used to treat different symptoms in different cats, here are some interesting remedies and their uses.

Apis Mellifica
(made from honey bee venom) can be used for allergies or to reduce swelling that occurs in acutely infected kidneys.

Calcarea Fluorica
(made from calcium fluoride, which helps harden bone structure) can be useful in treating hard lumps in tissues.

Kali Muriaticum
(made from potassium chloride) can help improve sluggish behaviour.

Natrum Muriaticum
(made from common salt, sodium chloride) is useful in treating thin, thirsty cats.

Nitricum Acidum
(made from nitric acid) is used for symptoms you would expect to see from contact with acids such as lesions, especially where the skin joins the linings of body orifices or openings such as the lips and nostrils.

Symphytum
(made from the herb Knitbone, *Symphytum officianale*) is used to encourage bones to heal.

Urtica Urens
(made from the common stinging nettle) is used in treating painful, irritating rashes.

HOMEOPATHIC REMEDIES FOR YOUR CAT

Symptom/Ailment	Possible Remedy
ABSCESSES	Ferrum Phosphoricum 1.5c, Ledum 1.5c, Echinacea Angustifolia, Silicea 3c
ALLERGIES	Apis Mellifica 30c, Astacus Fluviatilis 6c, Pulsatilla 30c, Urtica Urens 6c
ALOPAECIA	Alumina 30c, Lycopodium 30c, Sepia 30c, Thallium 6c
BLADDER PROBLEMS	Thlaspi Bursa Pastoris, Urtica Urens 3c, Apis Mellifica 1.5c, Rhus Toxicodendron 3c
CONSTIPATION	Alumina 6c, Carbo Vegetabilis 30c, Graphites 6c, Nitricum Acidum 30c, Silicea 6c
COUGHING	Aconitum Napellus 6c, Belladonna 30c, Hyoscyamus Niger 30c, Phosphorus 30c
DIARRHOEA	Arsenicum Album 30c, Aconitum Napellus 6c, Chamomilla 30c, Mercurius Corrosivus 30c
DRY EYE	Zincum Metallicum 30c
EAR MITES	Thyme (Thymus Vulgaris), Rosemary (Rosemarinus Officinalis), Rue (Ruta Gravedens)
EAR PROBLEMS	Aconitum Napellus 30c, Belladonna 30c, Hepar Sulphuris 30c, Tellurium 30c, Psorinum 200c
EYE PROBLEMS	Borax 6c, Aconitum Napellus 30c, Graphites 6c, Staphysagria 6c, Thuja Occidentalis 30c
FVR (Feline Viral Rhinotracheitis)	Ferrum Phosphoricum 3c, Kali Muriaticum 3c, Natrum Muriaticum 3c, Calcarea Phosphorica 3c
GLAUCOMA	Aconitum Napellus 30c, Apis Mellifica 6c, Phosphorus 30c
HEAT STROKE	Belladonna 30c, Gelsemium Sempervirens 30c, Sulphur 30c
HICCOUGHS	Cinchona Deficinalis 6c
INCONTINENCE	Argentum Nitricum 6c, Causticum 30c, Conium Maculatum 30c, Pulsatilla 30c, Sepia 30c
INSECT BITES	Apis Mellifica 30c, Cantharis 30c, Hypericum Perforatum 6c, Urtica Urens 30c
ITCHING	Alumina 30c, Arsenicum Album 30c, Carbo Vegetabilis 30c, Hypericum Perforatum 6c, Mezerium 6c, Sulphur 30c
LIVER PROBLEMS	Natrum Sulphuricum 1.5c, Bryonia 3c
MASTITIS	Apis Mellifica 30c, Belladonna 30c, Urtica Urens 1m
PENIS PROBLEMS	Aconitum Napellus 30c, Hepar Sulphuris Calcareum 30c, Pulsatilla 30c, Thuja Occidentalis 6c
RINGWORM	Plantago Major, Hydrastis Canadensis, Lavendula Vera, Sulphur 3c
UNDERWEIGHT CATS	Medicago Sativa, Calcarea Phosphorica 3c
VOMITING	Ipecac Root 1.5c, Ferrum Phosphoricum 3c

Recognising a Sick Cat

Unlike colicky babies and cranky children, our feline charges cannot tell us when they are feeling ill. Therefore, there are a number of signs that owners can identify to know that their cats are not feeling well.

Take note for physical manifestations such as:

- unusual, bad odour, including bad breath
- excessive moulting
- wax in the ears, chronic ear irritation
- oily, flaky, dull haircoat
- mucous, tearing or similar discharge in the eyes
- fleas or mites
- mucous in stool, diarrhoea
- sensitivity to petting or handling
- licking at paws, scratching face, etc.

Keep an eye out for behavioural changes as well including:

- lethargy, idleness
- lack of patience or general irritability
- lack of appetite, digestive problems
- phobias (fear of people, loud noises, etc.)
- strange behaviour, suspicion, fear
- coprophagia
- whimpering, crying

Get Well Soon

You don't need a DVR or a BVMA to provide good TLC to your sick or recovering cat, but you do need to pay attention to some details that normally wouldn't bother him. The following tips will aid Kitty's recovery and get him back on his paws again:

- Keep his space free of irritating smells, like heavy perfumes and air fresheners.
- Rest is the best medicine! Avoid harsh lighting that will prevent your cat from sleeping. Shade him from bright sunlight during the day and dim the lights in the evening.
- Keep the noise level down. Animals are more sensitive to sound when they are sick.

- Be attentive to any necessary temperature adjustments. A cat with a fever needs a cool room and cold liquids. A queen that is birthing or recovering from surgery will be more comfortable in a warm room, consuming warm liquids and food.
- You wouldn't send a sick child back to school early, so don't rush your cat back into a full routine until he seems absolutely ready.

USEFUL ADDRESSES

GREAT BRITAIN
The Governing Council of the Cat Fancy (GCCF)
4-6 Penel Orlieu, Bridgwater, Somerset, TA6 3PG
Email: GCCF_CATS@compuserve.com   Fax: 01278 446627 Tel: 01278 427575

The Cat Association of Britain
Mill House, Letcombe Regis, Oxon OX12 9JD   Tel: 01235 766543

EUROPE
Federation Internationale Feline (FIFe)
Gen. Sec: Ms Penelope Bydlinski.
Little Dene, Lenham Heath, Maidstone, Kent ME17 2BS, GB
Email: penbyd@compuserve.com   Fax: 1622 850193 Tel: 1622 850908

World Cat Federation
Hubertsrabe 280, D-45307, Essen, Germany
Email: wcf@nrw-online.de   Fax: 201-552747 Tel: 201-555724

AUSTRALIA
The Australian Cat Federation, Inc.
PO Box 3305, Port Adelaide, SA 5015
Email: acf@catlover.com   Fax: 08 8242 2767 Tel: 08 8449 5880

CANADA
Canadian Cat Association
220 Advance Boulevard, Suite 101, Brampton, Ontario L6T 4J5
Email: office@cca-afc.com   Fax: 99050 459-4023 Tel: 99060 459-1481

SOUTH AFRICA
Cat Federation of Southern Africa
PO Box 25, Bromhof 2154, Gauteng Province, Republic of South Africa

USA
American Cat Association
8101 Katherine Avenue, Panorama City, CA 91402
Fax: (818) 781-5340 Tel: (818) 781-5656

American Cat Fanciers Association
PO Box 203, Point Lookout, MO 65726
Email: info@acfacat.com   Fax: (417) 334-5540 Tel: (417) 334-5430

Cat Fanciers Association, Inc.
PO Box 1005, Manasquan, NJ 08736-0805
Email: cfa@cfainc.org   Fax: (732) 528-7391 Tel: (732) 528-9797

Cat Fanciers Federation
PO Box 661, Gratis, OH 45330
Email: Lalbert933@aol.com Fax: 937 787-4290 Tel: (937) 787-9009

The International Cat Association
PO Box 2684, Harlingen, TX 78551
Email: ticaeo@xanadu2.net Tel: (956) 428-8046